EASY
LEAF
TEA

Tea house recipes
to make at home

Timothy d'Offay
photography by Jan Baldwin

RYLAND PETERS & SMALL
LONDON • NEW YORK

CONTENTS

INTRODUCTION

A sea of green foam in a big black bowl, the sound of a spoon on the side of a much-loved mug, a thimble-sized cup cradling a highly scented elixir, and the taste of clay and sweet spices from a terracotta tumbler almost too hot to hold. Tea exists in so many forms and in so many different cultures around the world. Its remarkable journey from an obscure Chinese herb to the world's favourite beverage is partly due to tea's ability to be easily transported and then swiftly transformed into a delicious drink that relaxes and restores.

Because there are many ways of making tea, not to mention the many different types of tea – greens, blacks, oolongs, whites, and aged teas too – there is an almost infinite number of permutations and personal preferences. What a difference from the unhealthy mass-produced soft drinks that come ready-made in just a few flavours in a can or bottle designed to be thrown away after just one use. With tea you get choice – the choice of tea, any added ingredients and the vessel you want to drink from. Today people are discovering that brewing leaf tea is simple and many times tastier than bagged tea. Indeed, making tea may be the simplest form of cooking as it often involves just two ingredients and takes so little time. In this book I share the tea-making knowledge and ideas I have learnt since I first got enthused about leaf tea in Japan twenty-five years ago.

At the beginning of the book is a section on water and tea tools to make brewing easier, such as the hoop jug that helps you get the water temperature right for your green tea in an instant and with minimal fuss. Then, as well as traditional ways of making tea, we will explore new brewing methods such as Flow Brewing (see page 54) which involves brewing one tea through another to create an infusion and Ambient Tea (see pages 68–71), a way of making tea pair better with food. There is a chapter on delicious sparkling teas that I call Tea Sodas (see pages 80–87) and which you can make at home with just tea and a few other natural ingredients. Fresh Fruit Tea Quarters (see pages 88–101) are another

innovation, combining two things I love – tea and fresh fruit juice – to create a refreshing soft drink with only a quarter of the amount of sugar found in fruit juices.

One of most exciting recent developments in tea is the worldwide popularity of matcha both as a beverage and as an ingredient, liberating it from the refined world of the tea ceremony. In this book there are recipes to make the most of matcha and the other stoneground teas now available so you can learn to make new kinds of tasty drinks and desserts. So turn on your kettle, tune in to tea culture and drop those tasteless tea bags for something that's better for you and the planet.

WATER THE MAIN INGREDIENT

Water is the main ingredient of tea so selecting the right water is absolutely crucial to making good tea. In East Asia tea producers make their tea with their local water in mind and historically tea connoisseurs in Japan and China have been very fussy about finding the right water for brewing their tea. In the epic Qing dynasty novel *Dream of a Red Chamber*, for example, a Buddhist nun and tea connoisseur famously matches a tea with water from snow water collected from plum blossom branches several years previously. Obviously such pairings are neither practical nor ecological for most of us today.

In the UK, where there is both hard and soft water, matching tea to water rather than matching water to tea used to be an important part of the industry. Tea institutions, now long gone, used to suggest tea blends to mail order customers based on the water samples they would send in. The larger tea companies with national distribution also used to adjust their blends city by city across the country as they knew the water profile of each area. Today Taylors of Harrogate, a tea company in the north of England, still blends a black tea especially for the very hard water found in some parts of the UK. Thankfully most people have an affinity for the water they have grown up with or have drunk for many years. However, if your local tap water does not work with your favourite teas here are some things you can do.

If it is a chlorine issue, leaving the water to stand in a large jug, pitcher or a glass or ceramic container overnight can help. If this does not reduce the chlorine you may want to try one of the widely available charcoal filters for both your drinking and tea-brewing water. In my experience most water filters improve the clarity of the tea and will decrease any strong chlorine aromas but they can also make the tea seem a little lifeless.

As many people tend to prefer the taste of their local water, if you need to find a bottled water first look locally as it is also likely to be cheaper and of course be much more environmentally friendly. Ideally the mineral or spring water would be extracted sustainably and come to you in returnable/recyclable glass bottles or safe plastic (HDPE) containers. If none of your local bottled waters works with the teas you enjoy, as a last resort you could try these widely available bottled waters – Volvic, Vittel, and Highland Spring.

Once you have the right water, it should be stored in a cool place but it does not need to be refrigerated. Cold water has more oxygen which can make the water and later the tea taste better, just like a chilled soft drink always tastes more refreshing than a lukewarm one. As the boiling or reboiling of water reduces the oxygen, making the tea taste flat, be careful to use only the amount of water you need in your kettle and try to use fresh cold water for every new infusion.

Use cold water for your kettle as it contains more oxygen, which means the tea you make will be more delicious (left).

TEA WARE ALL YOU'LL EVER NEED

KETTLE

We had a kettle; we let it leak:
Our not repairing made it worse.
We haven't had any tea for a week …
The bottom is out of the Universe

Kipling's lines are a humorous reminder of the importance of a kettle in a tea drinker's life. I have few recommendations for buying a kettle other than to suggest you look for a metal kettle with as little plastic inside the kettle as possible both for potential health issues and because certain plastic kettles can have a distinctive smell.

A Japanese iron kettle or tetsubin is a once-in-a-lifetime investment, but be warned they require a dedicated owner as after every use they should be emptied of water otherwise they can rust and develop holes, just like Kipling's kettle. These handmade iron kettles do not have the enamel interiors that the popular teapot tetsubin have but instead iron interiors which fans believe purifies the water and gives the tea a better aroma and texture.

A more affordable choice is a temperature-controlled kettle. There are many good steel ones available, including ones developed for coffee specialists with goose neck spouts which makes pouring more accurate. One word of warning about temperature-controlled kettles – they can, over time, lose the accuracy of their internal temperature thermometer, sometimes due to limescale building up within the kettle. We try not to descale our kettle as descaling in the short term will effect the taste of the tea. However if any limescale cannot be removed by hand, lemon or lime juice as well as vinegar are effective natural descalers. Just cover the area you wish to descale with the juice or vinegar and soak for over an hour, then add water and boil the kettle. Pour off all the hot water from the kettle and rinse it several times with cold water before boiling once again, and then you should be ready to use your kettle again.

TEAPOT

The teapot's design has changed little since Chinese craftsmen first produced large numbers of Yixing teapots in the early 1500s. The teapot boom was a response to an early Ming dynasty emperor decreeing that more tea should be made in the loose leaf form. Up until then a lot of tea was pressed into cakes and bricks, some of which also had a scented wax around them and this tea was often ground and whisked in a bowl like matcha used in the Japanese tea ceremony.

Yixing teapots and other clay teapots are still produced today and their attraction for tea aficionados is the way they can influence a tea's texture and aromas – it's a bit like listening to music with a sophisticated stereo system where you can alter the treble and the bass to suit your taste.

The most common clay in Yixing is a reddy-brown colour and the shape and colour influenced many western teapots, including the iconic British Brown Betty. The advantage of a brown or darker glazed pot is that the tea stains, both inside and outside the pot, do not show.

A selection of teapots and kettles in a diversity of materials. Why not see if you have a teapot or kettle hidden away in a kitchen cupboard you can use before you decide to buy a new one? (right)

This page, clockwise from top:
Chashaku scoop, Shino chawan,
and chasen whisk on the tray.
Opposite page, from the top:
Hoop scoop and hoop jug,
Fairness jug and gaiwan,
and a Yixing teapot.

The material of a teapot also is worth a little consideration. If durability is very important to you, porcelain or bone china are tougher and less likely to chip than other forms of pottery and glass. Glass has many fans who enjoy seeing the colour of the tea, some can even judge when their tea is brewed to the strength they like by the infusion's colour. If you buy a glass teapot try to choose one with a shorter spout which is less likely to break. To be able to enjoy the colour of the tea in your glass pot you may have to regularly clean the pot with something stronger than just detergent. I use bicarbonate of soda or denture cleaning tablets with warm water to shift stubborn stains on teapots.

The size of a teapot is an important consideration. While you can make just one cup in a large teapot, it is much easier to use a smaller one so do choose a pot according to how much tea you normally brew. Also, if you like to make your tea strong and over several infusions, smaller teapots under 200 ml/7 oz. are ideal. Another design feature to check is whether the pot has something to catch tea leaves when you pour the liquid tea out. Many modern teapots only have a large hole where the body meets the spout which is fine if you are using teabags but not for leaf tea as most of the leaves will end up in your cup or your strainer. Teapots with a built-in cylindrical filter or strainer that can be removed are practical for removing leaves, but these pots severely limit the movement of the leaves and therefore will not brew as good a pot of tea as those without such restriction of movement. Although I have listed some things you might want to consider when choosing a teapot, do also be guided by your instincts as this very special object is likely to be at the heart of hospitality in your home so it has to feel right.

GAIWAN AND OTHER INFUSERS

I am a big fan of these small easy-to-use and very easy-to-clean brewers often made out of durable porcelain. The gaiwan revolutionised leaf tea drinking in China as it was cheaper than a teapot and was both a brewer and a cup. The Japanese version of a gaiwan is called a shiboridashi and has a very short spout to pour the tea into another vessel or cup. Other infusers like hohin or modern versions of these brewers also offer a quick and easy way to brew leaf tea. Glass travelling versions with a mesh infuser are another addition to your tea tools worth considering, especially if you want to try making tea sodas.

HOOP JUG

If you enjoy teas that are brewed with lower water temperatures like green teas, the hoop jug is a really useful tool. I developed it as the simplest and quickest way to get the water temperature right for tea brewing. All you need is a glass jug/pitcher and some rubber bands or a marker pen. To calibrate it to the water temperature(s) you want you will need use a thermometer or some time to work out which levels work best for your teas. As a basic guide, if you fill the jug a third full with cold water and then two-thirds with boiling water the water temperature is approximately 70°C/160°F, which is good for many Japanese green teas. If you use a quarter of cold water to three quarters boiling the temperature should be about 80°C/175°F, which is suitable for many Chinese green teas and some greenish First Flush Darjeelings. Using the rubber bands or the marker pen, record your personal preferences so you'll never need to wait for your water to cool or use a thermometer to make certain teas again.

FAIRNESS JUG

This jug is a fairly recent Taiwanese invention for Gong Fu-style tea, which allows you to decant all the infusion from a teapot into a jug/pitcher. The tea is then shared among the guests. The advantage over the traditional method of pouring tea from the pot to one cup then another is that everyone drinking from a fairness jug shares the same strength tea.

CHASEN AND CHASHAKU

A chasen is the Japanese bamboo whisk and chashaku the bamboo scoop used to make matcha. The most famous place for their production is in Takayama, a village in Nara prefecture where some of the families who live there have been making them for twenty generations. Their superior skill as well as their careful aging of the bamboo makes Takayama chasen highly sought after and expensive. Much cheaper chasen and chashaku are now made in China and are perfectly fine for everyday use.

Before use, briefly soak the chasen in warm water. After use carefully wash the chasen's prongs in cold water, gently pat dry and then air dry, ideally horizontally on a nail or upside down on a clothes rail. For those concerned about keeping their chasen in peak condition you could buy a chasen holder to keep the shape of the prongs perfect.

CHAWAN

A chawan is the tea bowl used to whisk matcha in and drink the tea from. These bowls are often from Japan but famous chawan styles are also made in Korea, Vietnam and China. They come in all shapes, colours, clays and sizes to suit different occasions and seasons. Judge a chawan not just by the way it looks but also by the way it feels. Hold it to assess whether its size and shape feels right and put its lip to your lips to see how drinking from it will be. If you cannot find a chawan you love, feel free to use another bowl. For those who are not natural matcha makers, bowls with high sides make whisking a tea with lots of foam easier than a shallow bowl.

SCOOPS AND SPOONS

The tea bag is a terrible invention for brewing tea but a brilliant piece of portion control. Before tea bags, we used tea scoops, spoons and scales to portion out the leaf tea we needed. They all can still be useful measures until you get familiar enough to work out the correct quantity of your favourite teas by sight.

Another useful tool is what I have nicknamed the hoop scoop which, like the hoop jug, uses volume as a measure. As two teas of the same weight can be very different in volume, the hoop scoop allows you to measure and mark with rubber bands or a pen just the right amount of tea you'll need on a small glass jug. The advantage over spoons, scoops and scales is how accurate and quick the hoop scoop is to use.

CADDIES

Air, heat, light, moisture and time are the enemies of most teas so an air-tight pack or caddy is essential. If you are using a new tin you may want to test its air tightness by pouring water into it and seeing if any leaks. If it doesn't leak, dry the container very carefully and then season the tin with a little tea for a day or two before filling up the tin with tea. Many materials like metal, wood, lacquer and plastic will have a residual smell, so seasoning the container with a little tea can help get rid of the slight smell of the material. Clear glass containers, although visually appealing, should be avoided unless the glass is dark coloured as light can dramatically change the colour and flavour of the tea.

This page: A traditional Brown Betty teapot with a Rockingham brown glaze together with a teacup. Opposite page: A selection of tea and kitchen strainers.

If you are using bags or packs be aware that plastic is permeable, and only packs made with a material that has a layer of metal will protect your tea from oxygen and light. If they do not come with a zip-lock function, use a strong bulldog/foldback clip to seal them or ideally store the pack inside a tin or container.

Tea should be stored in a cool place but refrigerators are not suitable because they often contain food with strong smells and condensation can form after the pack is taken out of the refrigerator.

STRAINERS

If you have a teapot with a built-in strainer you may not need an everyday strainer, though you may find one useful for some of the recipes in this book. One consideration is to choose a strainer with a deep net. When travelling, a deep strainer can be used for infusing your own leaf tea in a cup, offering a taste of home rather than the tea bag a hotel might offer.

CUPS

With Peter Ting, a celebrated ceramics designer, I created an unusual range of three tea cups which is now in the permanent collection of London's Victoria and Albert Museum. It focused on three difference characteristics you might look for in tea – texture, fragrance and balance. The cups could be used for any type of tea but were originally created with the main types of tea in mind so the texture cup is for green, the fragrance cup for oolong and the balance cup for black and dark teas like puerh.

What many people found fascinating was how different the taste and experience of drinking the same tea in the three different cups was. Like using a yixing clay teapot to personalise the tea, drinking tea from different shaped cups allows you to emphasize your personal preferences. There has also been research to show that your tea tastes better out of a special cup which may have sentimental value or feel culturally right for the tea you like to drink. All I would like to suggest is that you experiment with drinking tea out of different cups to see which ones enhance your experience of the tea. Hopefully instead of having just one favoured cup, you will find you have a selection of cups you adore, one for each of your favourite teas.

WATER THERMOMETER

I prefer old-style mechanical metal thermometers (a cooking one should work fine) as they tend to be more robust than digital thermometers. Remember to fully immerse the thermometer in the hot water to get an accurate reading.

SINK STRAINER

A sink mesh bowl or basket is perfect for catching the leaves so you can use them for compost or as a room deodorant (they are great at absorbing bad smells).

1
EASY LEAF TEA LOOSE LEAF LIFE

As a child I remember occasionally making loose leaf tea. Once at a friend's house I was tasked with brewing some Lapsang Souchong and I still have a strong memory of the tea's unusual sweet smokiness. Most of the time though, I would make strong black tea with a tea bag in a mug and drink it with milk like most Brits do. My mother bought a particular popular brand so my relationship to tea was with that brand rather than with tea itself as it is hard to relate to something in a sealed paper bag which you can barely see, smell or taste.

My narrow black and white tea world only came to end when I went to study in the ancient Japanese city of Kyoto in my early twenties. For the first time in my life I was completely surrounded by tea, from the tea fields south of the city to the tea art, architecture and culture of the tea ceremony which I studied for a short time. At home, my homestay family also made all their tea loose leaf in a teapot. My fellow students, who mainly came from other Asian countries, also shared their tea so through them I started to enjoy tea from Taiwan, China and Korea. All their teas were loose leaf and it made me realise that there were many more kinds of teas available loose leaf than in tea bags. So not only did a loose leaf life offer better flavours and more delicious flavours, but also, seemingly, a tea for every mood and moment.

TEA HOW A LITTLE LEAF BECAME BIG

The tea plant is a camellia with small white flowers similar to the ornamental camellias you find in gardens around the world. Like most other camellias it is thought to have originated in the sub-Himalayan area that includes north-east India, Burma, Laos and south-west China. In this area ancient tea trees grow to a great height and a great age – the oldest are believed to be almost two thousand years old. As its properties became valued, tea seems to have travelled north to Sichuan province in China where the earliest tea cultivation took place. One of the ways of making tea at this time was to boil it with things such as ginger, spring onion/scallion, orange peel, jujube fruit, dogwood berries and peppermint. Lu Yu, the author of the first book on tea written in the Tang dynasty (618–907 AD) describes how tea could come in many forms – loose, powdered and cake formats. He was scathing about the adding of any ingredients other than a little salt and carefully detailed his preferred way of preparing tea which included selecting special water for tea.

China's next dynasty, the Song Dynasty saw tea's popularity increase as the drink reached almost all levels of Chinese society. Tea was now considered to be one of daily necessities of life in China, the other necessities being firewood, rice, oil, salt, sauce and vinegar. A new, simpler way of making tea by whisking powdered tea in a bowl may have been partly responsible for this new boom. This new tea also inspired amazing kinds of ceramic glazes to show off the beauty of the tea. Soon both the new tea and tea bowls were being brought to neighbouring countries by foreign monks who had studied at Chinese Buddhist temples and then returned home.

When this style of tea reached Japan it gradually transformed into what we now know as the tea ceremony.

The Ming Dynasty brought more change to Chinese society and to tea. The first Mongol emperor of this dynasty, Hongwu Emperor, started the process by banning the making of moulded tea cakes for his tribute tea. It is unclear whether the emperor did this to reduce the corruption in the trade of tribute tea or to encourage others to enjoy the pure taste of loose leaf tea untainted by camphor oil and wax which was used to press these cakes. One the emperor's sons, Zhu Quan (1378–1448) also made a significant contribution by writing a tea-brewing manual which further encouraged the consumption of loose leaf tea.

In Yixing, China's most famous teapot production area, earlier shards of teapot-shaped vessels have been found but there was no significant production until the early 1500s. Yixing teapots and the invention of the gaiwan lidded cup, which could be used for brewing and drinking from, finally gave leaf tea the tools it needed to reach an even wider audience.

Soon the world was coming to China, attracted by its incredible riches and unique products like silk, porcelain and tea. The Portuguese, who established the island of Macao as their base in the 1550s, were the first Europeans to trade with China, followed by the Dutch. The Portuguese and Dutch elites were also the first Europeans to appreciate tea from the early 17th century onwards. Although tea reached England in the 1650s, the Portuguese princess Catherine of Braganza who married Charles II in 1662 really sparked the trend for tea. Soon afterwards the newly established East India Company started trading with

A tea plant in bloom (right).

China and amongst the things they imported was tea with tea pots and other ceramics often used as ballast for their ships.

In 1699 John Ovington, who worked for the East India Company, wrote an essay on tea. Ovington describes 'the method the Chinese use in preparing of tea' by putting it in 'ovens, or in kilns, or to expose it to the sun' and 'by frying it twice or oftner in a pan'. Once out of the pan 'it is roll'd with the hand upon a table till it curls. By this means the leaves contract such a dryness and hardness, as it enables them to retain their virtue for many years'. He also describes several types of Chinese tea including a green tea with a fragrant smell and 'bitterish sweet taste' and a Wuyi tea which had black leaves and the Chinese believed had the potential for healing and preventing a disease. The Wuyi tea Ovington described was probably a roasted oolong (oolong literally means black dragon, probably on account of the look of its leaves) but in Europe Wuyi or Bohea tea was considered a black tea.

By the early 19th century the English East India Company was buying over 11 million kilos of tea a year and paying for it with silver which they acquired through the sale of opium they grew in India. Since the East India Company wanted to break China's monopoly on tea production they commissioned plant hunters, the most famous being Robert Fortune, to go to China's premier tea-growing areas like Wuyi and take tea seeds and plants so they could establish and manufacture tea in India. In this way Fortune's seeds and seedlings from the Wuyi area helped start the plantations in Darjeeling where the climate suited the Chinese tea varietal.

In other areas of India, the Chinese tea varietal (*Camellia sinensis var. sinensis*) did not prosper. Luckily for the British they already had indigenous Indian tea in the far north-eastern state of Assam. It had been recognised in 1823 by a Scotsman Robert Bruce who learnt about the tea from the Singhpo people but it was not developed until later as the Chinese varietal was considered superior. However, being the local variety, *Camellia sinensis var. assamica* was better suited to the hotter more humid conditions and soon large parts of Assam's jungles had been cleared and planted with the varietal. This varietal produced a more robust, stronger cup which proved popular in Britain – so much so that the British started growing this tea in other parts of its empire, ensuring the spread of tea to south India, Sri Lanka and Africa. Today, although China and India continue to be some of the largest tea producers in the world, tea is grown on every continent with the exception of Antarctica.

This page: A misty tea field with shade trees in the Nilgiri mountains in southern India. Opposite page: Tea picking on a small farm, part of the Mineral Springs Cooperative in Darjeeling, northern India.

TYPES OF TEA

Whether a tea is a green tea or a black tea is determined by the processing, not by the type of tea plant. Though certain varietals and cultivars are undoubtedly more suited to certain tea types, you can make any type of tea from any tea varietal or cultivar.

After the tea leaves are plucked they begin to wilt. Once the leaves reach the factory this wilting process, or withering as it is known in the tea world, is controlled by the producer. Withering can be done inside or outside in troughs or on trays, and the purpose is to reduce the moisture in the leaf by up to a half and also develop good flavour in the final tea.

Next come the stages of processing which define what type of tea it will be. Think of how the inside of an apple starts to brown when it is cut – a similar sort of oxidization happens when tea leaves' cell walls are broken by rolling or breaking up the leaves, which is what is done to oolong and black tea leaves. Typically oolong teas are oxidized somewhere between 10% and about 70% and black teas are oxidized 70% upwards. During the stage of oxidization the tea leaves yield amazing floral and fruity aromas which help the tea producer know when the right degree of oxidization has been reached. Then the leaves are heat-treated to de-enzyme them and halt any further oxidization. The tea may then be rolled and dried until it has a moisture content of less than 5% which enables it to be stable and be stored for a long time, a bit like freeze-dried foods can be.

With white and green teas this process of initiating oxidization through breaking the tea leaves' cell walls is skipped. In the case of green tea, oxidization is stopped by heat-treating the leaves by firing them in a wok for a traditional Chinese green tea or steaming the leaves for most Japanese green tea. There may be rolling of the leaves to bring out more flavour to the tea before the tea is dried. With the white tea there is no rolling or firing and the leaves are just gently sun dried or machine dried. This lack of processing and rolling explains why white tea tends to have more delicate flavours than other tea types.

Long Jing, a famous Chinese green tea, being handmade in a wok. The firing initially stops oxidization and then the hot wok is used to shape and dry the tea leaves (above).

20 LEAF TEAS TO TRY

1 SILVER NEEDLE WHITE TEA

White tea became a fashion not so long ago and now is much more widely available than it once was. This should be a good thing but unfortunately many of the teas sold are underwhelming.

A good-quality Silver Needle (Yin Zhen) tea should give a subtle sweetness together with fruit aromas like melon or pear, sometimes with gentle vegetal flavours too. The texture for such a light tea can also be surprisingly rich and creamy. Made from the early spring downy buds of the Da Bai (Great White) cultivar, it traditionally comes from the areas around the mountain town of Fuding in Fujian province. As well as recently harvested white teas, aged whites teas pressed into cakes are also a speciality of the Fuding area. The aging over several years is believed to develop the tea's medicinal qualities and gives it a darker colour when brewed and an Oriental Beauty oolong-like taste.

150 ml/5 oz. water at 90 ˚C/195 ˚F, 3 g tea
1st infusion 3 minutes – 2nd infusion 2 minutes

2 LONG JING

China's most famous and favourite green tea is now made in many tea-growing areas across the country. However the real Long Jing or Dragon Well tea is Xihu Long Jing (West Lake Long Jing) that comes only from the hills just outside beautiful Hangzhou city, near Shanghai. Produced in late March to late April, the earliest production is particularly prized, especially the pre-Qing Ming tea produced before the Qing Ming tomb-sweeping festival in early April which can be extremely expensive. As the temperature rises, more and more tea is produced so the price falls, but even later harvested teas from the Xihu area are not cheap. Real Long Jing has a light vegetal, sweet chestnut flavour with a very long aftertaste. Like many of the best other Chinese green teas, like Bi Luo Chun, Mao Feng, Mao Jian and Taiping Houkui, it can and should be made with very hot water and will make many infusions.

150 ml/5 oz. water at 85 ˚C/185 ˚F, 3 g tea
1st infusion 1 minute and 15 seconds – 2nd infusion 30 seconds

3 SENCHA

Well over half the tea produced in Japan every spring is sencha with its rich grassy vegetal flavours. Unlike Chinese green teas, sencha is steamed and there are two main styles – futsumushi (normal or traditional steaming which is for about 30 seconds) and the sweeter greener fukamushi (deep steaming which is for over a minute). Yame in Fukuoka prefecture, Hon-yama and Kawane in Shizuoka prefecture and Uji in Kyoto prefecture produce the most prized sencha but there are remarkable teas from elsewhere. If you cannot taste the tea before buying, shiny dark green leaves are a sign of a quality tea. Sencha teas are often blended for a particular taste or price point by the grower or the tea merchant. The main cultivar used is Yabukita which accounts for over 70% of Japan's tea. It is a cold-resistant, high-yielding plant that produces a well-balanced smooth tea.

150 ml/5 oz. water at 70˚C/160˚F, 5 g tea
1st infusion 1 minute – 2nd infusion almost instant

4 GYOKURO

If Chinese teas are celebrated for their aroma, Japanese teas are known for their texture and there is no tea that can match Gyokuro's thick, rich texture. Indeed it can sometimes seem more like a culinary delicacy than a beverage when it is served luke warm in tiny cups. Traditionally shaded for three weeks with a canopy of reeds and sticky rice plant stalks, nowadays plastic sheeting is usually used to develop the sweetness and umami in the tea. This occurs because the shading reduces photosynthesis in the leaves and the formation of astringent catechins in the plant while increasing the amino acid L-theanine which gives sweetness and texture to the tea. As it is a tea to savour drop by drop, one modern method to enjoy it is to take an ice cube and place it on the top of a bed of Gyokuro in a hohin or other small infuser and drink the tea little by little as it slowly melts.

85 ml/3 oz. water at 50˚C/120˚F, 6 g tea
1st infusion 1 minute and 30 seconds – 2nd infusion 45 seconds

5 GENMAICHA

Genmaicha is a mixture of some late harvest sencha green tea and roasted rice – usually mochi rice (sticky rice). Often some of the rice kernels pop so they look like popcorn. A good example of the tea is very comforting to drink and has a lovely balance between the grassy green flavour of the tea and the toasted nutty flavour from the rice. The tea is thought to have originated among poor farmers who used rice to make their precious tea go further. Today it is popular throughout Japan, especially in the cities because it works well with water that is chlorinated, and it is easy to brew with water just off the boil so it is easier to prepare than sencha that needs cooler water. Another advantage of Genmaicha is that it is lower in caffeine than other Japanese green teas as the tea is from a later harvest and its tea percentage is reduced by the rice.

150 ml/5 oz. water at 85°C/185°F, 4 g tea
1st infusion 30 seconds – 2nd infusion almost instant

6 HOJICHA

Hojicha is a Japanese roasted green tea with wonderful sweet tobacco and hay-like aromas. It is thought to have been invented by a canny tea merchant in Kyoto city in the early 20th century who wanted to find a use for some older green tea that was losing its flavour. By roasting it for a short time at a high temperature of around 200°C/400°F – much higher than the Chinese roast their oolong teas at – the merchant found the tea developed delicious sweetness and was easier on the stomach than many Japanese teas. Today you can still see and smell Hojicha and its local variety Kyobancha being roasted in Kyoto where most homes and restaurants serve it everyday. Hojicha can be found in many different variations around Japan, some using just the tea stalks (Kuki-Hojicha) and others with much darker, almost coffee-like roasts.

150 ml/5 oz. water at 90°C/195°F, 2 g tea
1st infusion 1 minute – 2nd infusion 30 seconds

7 JASMINE PEARLS

The Chinese are masters of scenting tea with fresh flowers, and jasmine is their most famous scented tea. Jasmine pearls are a relatively recent development which have largely replaced Yin Hao jasmine, which is also made with the young spring leaves and downy silver buds as the grandest jasmine tea. The difference between the two is the careful hand-rolling of the pearl tea into little balls which, like other jasmine teas, are then scented when summer comes and the jasmine plants are in bloom. The best grades of jasmine teas are scented up to ten times with fresh jasmine flowers so the aroma is fully absorbed by the tea. Jasmine pearls are particularly easy to use as the individual pearls can be counted rather than weighed before brewing. Indeed many people enjoy jasmine pearls by putting five or so in a cup, pouring on hot water and drinking as the pearls slowly unfurl.

150 ml/5 oz. water at 85°C/185°F, 4 g tea
1st infusion 2 minutes – 2nd infusion 30 seconds

8 HIGH MOUNTAIN OOLONG

High altitudes and colder climates slow the growth of plants and expose them to more UV light which helps produce more aromatic tea. High mountain Oolongs, or Gaoshan teas as they known as in Taiwan, are grown at altitudes from about 1000–2600 metres/3000–8500 feet and are known for sweet, fruity and floral aromas and sometimes a refreshing menthol-like kick. Though some high mountain tea farming had been going on for over 50 years, it was not until the booming 1980s economy that the explosion of tea farming on the island's highest mountains really began. The most famous mountains are Lishan, Alishan, Yushan and Shan Lin Xi. There are excellent teas grown on lesser well-known mountains too and they are less likely to be forgeries which bedevil the high mountain category so much that the top competition winning teas always come in individually numbered tins with special limited edition holographic stickers. Wash the leaves with 95°C/205°F water for 20 seconds, pour off the water, wait for 2 minutes, then brew the first proper infusion.

150 ml/5 oz. water at 95°C/205°F, 6 g tea
Wash + 1st infusion 45 seconds – 2nd infusion 20–30 seconds

9 TAIWANESE GREEN OOLONG

As well as the high mountain teas, the lower elevations of central Taiwan make wonderful fragrant ball-rolled green oolongs with different cultivars like Si Ji Chun (Four Seasons Like Spring) or Cui Yu (Jade Green). These lower grown oolongs, usually grown at around 500–600 meters/1600–2000 feet, offer great value for money because their yield is greater than higher grown teas and many are mechanically harvested. They may also be more environmentally friendly because excessive high mountain farming has been blamed for landslides in part due to the deforestation and increase in soil water content that farming brings. My favourite lower grown oolongs come from the hard-working and betel nut chewing farmers of Ming Jian town in Nantou county. Their sweet floral oolongs with jasmine and other white flower fragrances make many infusions. And if you ever want a variation, why not try one of the roasted versions of these fabulous teas. Wash the leaves with 95°C/205°F water for 20 seconds, pour off the water, wait for 2 minutes, then brew the first proper infusion.

150 ml/5 oz. water at 90°C/195°F, 6 g tea
Wash + 1st infusion 45 seconds – 2nd infusion 30 seconds

10 PHOENIX OOLONG

The high mountains around Chaozhou city in Guangdong produce oolongs with incredible floral and fruity flavours. Though theories about the local flora influencing wine flavours seems to have been dismissed, my take on why local flavours like lychee, rambutan, certain flowers as well as the famous local honey are in the teas is that the tea makers select tea trees that exhibit the local flavours they know and love and as well as working to mimic them through their tea processing. On the most revered mountain, Wudong shan, the oldest trees are many hundreds of years old and some are the mother trees for the modern clonal versions of the ten or so different Phoenix Oolong varieties which are named after the flower fragrances they evoke like magnolia, ginger and osmanthus. The most popular and widely available Phoenix Dan Cong Oolong is Mi Lan Xiang or Honey Orchid Fragrance. Wash the leaves with 95°C/205°F water for 20 seconds, pour off the water, wait for 2 minutes, then brew the first proper infusion.

150 ml/5 oz. water at 90°C/195°F, 6 g tea
Wash + 1st infusion 30 seconds – 2nd infusion 30 seconds

11 ORIENTAL BEAUTY

A Taiwanese oolong tea famous for its perfume-like aroma. Little leafhopper insects bite the leaves, causing the plant to produce a defensive chemical which, when processed, produces the tea's unique aroma. Oriental Beauty is produced in the north of Taiwan in Beipu and Miaoli where the prize-winning teas are soon snapped up by rich local buyers despite their unbelievably high prices, so very little of the best grades leave Taiwan. Luckily lower grades of Oriental Beauty (Dongfang Meiren) – sometimes also called White Tip (Bai Hao) oolong – are exported and are delicious examples of highly oxidized oolongs. These teas are often reminiscent of aromatic muscatel Darjeeling Second Flush teas. However, inexpensive Oriental Beauty Oolongs never have the incredible complex flower and fruit aromas, honey-like sweetness, nor endless infusions that a prize-winning one has. Wash the leaves with 95°C/205°F water for 20 seconds, pour off the water, wait for 2 minutes then brew the first proper infusion.

150 ml/5 oz. water at 90°C/195°F, 5 g tea
Wash + 1st infusion 1 minute – 2nd infusion 30 seconds

12 WUYI OOLONG

The Wuyi mountains in the north of Fujian are the likely birthplace of oolong tea. Here they roll lengthwise and heavily roast the partially oxidized leaves so some of the leaves look like a 'black dragon' which is the translation of 'oolong' probably because of the leaves' shape. The teas are also known as yancha, or cliff tea, because the tea grows in the decomposing rock soil, giving the tea a special minerality that other areas outside the inner zone cannot match. The most famous tea or tea trees from Wuyi are the legendary old trees of Da Hong Pao that are visited by hundreds of thousands of tourists every year. Tea has been cloned from these old trees but I prefer Shui Xian and Rou Gui which can have a combination of peach and other stone fruit flavours together with rose-like floral aromas and a rich woody roast.

150 ml/5 oz. water at 90°C/195°F, 6 g tea
1st infusion 30 seconds – 2nd infusion 45 seconds

13 LAPSANG

If you have been drinking coarse generic Lapsang, it is a bit of a shock when you drink the real thing. Lapsang from the Tong Mu area of the Wuyi mountains is smooth and rich with a gentle smokiness reminiscent of a fine Scotch whisky with a fruity smoked bacon flavour going on too. There are lots of legends about how this tea came to be smoked, but my guess is that as this was an export tea they were looking for a way to make it suitable and robust enough for the long sea journeys to the markets in the West. Seeing the nearby roasted Wuyi oolongs, which were popular in the West as 'black' teas, they thought of another way of preserving tea and tried gently smoking it with green pine wood. Whatever the real origin, Lapsang Souchong has been a popular tea since the 19th century and continues to be world's finest smoked tea.

150 ml/5 oz. water at 95°C/205°F, 4 g tea
1st infusion 1 minute – 2nd infusion 30 seconds
2 cup teapot 350 ml/12 oz. water at 95°C/205°F, 5 g tea – 2 minutes

14 KEEMUN

In 1875 China's answer to the British production of tea in India was to produce a black tea of such quality that the West could not ignore it. Grown by the same farmers who also make the famous Mao Feng green tea on Huangshan mountain in Anhui province, Keemun or Qimen quickly won many awards and was acknowledged as a classic black tea. Its malty, fruity flavours with a touch of leather and chocolate made it popular as a single origin tea and as a major component of the first breakfast blends. Although it was originally an export tea, recently the Chinese have been discovering premium versions of Keemun and other fine black teas from their own country, like Jin Jun Mei from Wuyi. These teas tend to be comprised of the earliest buds and like many of the finest Chinese teas have exquisite complex aromas.

150 ml/5 oz. water at 95°C/205°F, 4 g tea
1st infusion 1 minute + 15 seconds – 2nd infusion 45 seconds
2 cup teapot 350 ml/12 oz. water 95°C/205°F, 5 g tea – 2 minutes

15 DARJEELING FIRST FLUSH

As Darjeeling was originally planted with tea that Robert Fortune had taken from the famous oolong area of Wuyi in China, it is no surprise that Darjeeling teas are a little oolong like. In most of Asia, tea hibernates through winter as it is too cold for the plant to produce new leaves or 'flush' as it is called in the industry. As spring comes and the temperature rises, the first teas are made in Darjeeling usually in March. Many of these first flush teas do not look or taste like a black tea. Their yellow-green colour and floral and tropical fruit aromas are more reminscient of a green oolong tea, but because they are processed partly like black tea I have seen them described as 'partially oxidized black teas'. Whatever they are, they can be a glorious symphony of spring flavours which explains why there is a race amongst many tea merchants to see who can import and start selling them the earliest every year.

150 ml/5 oz. water at 85 °C/185 °F, 4 g tea
1st infusion 1 minute – 2nd infusion 30–45 seconds
2 cup teapot 350 ml/12 oz. water at 85 °C/185 °F, 5 g tea – 2 minutes

16 DARJEELING SECOND FLUSH

Darjeeling means 'land of Indra's thunderbolt', and the name is highly appropriate if you consider that during the monsoon it can rain more in just one month than it does in an entire year in London. Before the monsoon rains come in June and literally wash the flavour out of the tea, Darjeeling produces some of the world's most enjoyable black teas. If you look at the tea leaves after brewing you will still see a few flecks of green leaf that show that the tea is not fully oxidized but this level of oxidization is partly responsible for the tea's lovely aroma. While a First Flush might be rolled for 15 minutes and allowed to oxidize for 15 minutes, a Second Flush may be rolled for about an hour and allowed to oxidize for an hour before being fired. A decent second flush tea should have a good balance between astringency and sweetness with woody pine-like tones and sometimes a Muscat grape aroma.

150 ml/5 oz. water at 95 °C/205 °F, 4 g tea
1st infusion 1 minute – 2nd infusion 45 seconds
2 cup teapot 350 ml/12 oz. water at 95 °C/205 °F, 5 g tea – 2 minutes

17 ASSAM

The fertile gently undulating landscape of Assam is the heartland of India's tea industry. Established through the toil of tea workers, tens of thousands of whom died of malaria while clearing jungle and establishing plantations in the 19th century, Assam now produces about half of India's tea. Sadly most of the tea is CTC (Crush, Tear and Curl) which is a process that chops up tea leaves to promote fast oxidization of the tea and shapes the tea into small spheres of tea that brew quickly – it is the tea you often find in tea bags. As CTC dominates the Indian market, many Assam factories no longer produce whole leaf teas which is a great shame as the best Second Flush Assams are a joy. These tippy teas made in May and June before the monsoon have a strong malty character and sometimes an almost red wine-like fruity flavour. Assam tea and milk is a match made in heaven.

2 cup teapot 350 ml/12 oz. water at 90 °C/195 °F, 7 g tea – 2 minutes

18 LOWER ELEVATION CEYLON

Lower elevation black teas from the Ruhuna and Sabaragamuwa tea districts often get overlooked when people look for teas from Sri Lanka but these teas are great everyday drinking teas. Both areas are in the south of the island and the estates are usually located inland from the coast in gentle hills. The districts also include the Unesco protected Sinharaja Forest Reserve which is Sri Lanka's last remaining tropical rainforest. The warm and wet climate produces lots of tea which is why these lower elevation teas account for nearly half the island's tea. Ruhuna and Sabaragamuwa teas are usually strong with a lovely spicy characteristic. Brewed lightly they are excellent teas for drinking without milk but if brewed strongly, these low elevation teas work wonderfully with milk too. Areas to look out for include Galle, Ratnapura, Sinharaja and Matara.

2 cup teapot 350 ml/5 oz. water at 90 °C/195 °F, 6 g tea – 2 minutes

19 HIGH GROWN CEYLON NUWARA ELIYA

Nuwara Eliya, famous for its tea and its tourism, is known locally as 'Little England' on account of its temperate climate. It is a strange patchwork of mountain tea plantations, deep green forestry, grand old English-style buildings and lots of colourful flowers, both in gardens and commercial nurseries. Nuwara Eliya tea is also a patchwork of olive green, beige, copper and bronze colours that produce a light smooth tea with cypress aromas and a dry rather than an astringent quality. The area has the highest average elevation of all tea-growing districts in Sri Lanka with estates often producing tea at around 2000 m/6500 feet. Nuwara Eliya enjoys its quality season from January to about April when there is the least rainfall and the most sunshine during the day, followed by cold nights which concentrate the flavours in this yellowy orange tea.

2 cup teapot 350 ml/12 oz. water at 90 °C/195 °F, 6 g tea – 2 minutes

20 HIGH GROWN CEYLON UVA

Uva is a mountainous tea-growing area that Sir Thomas Lipton helped promote around the world. He established the Dambatenne tea estate there in 1890 as part of a massive expansion of tea production in Sri Lanka that followed the decimation of the coffee industry by the coffee rust virus in the second half of the 19th century.

The dry season in Uva comes with the Cachan or Kachan wind that blows through the Uva area from July to September. The drying wind reduces moisture and concentrates the oils in the leaves of the Uva tea plants which leads to subtle wintergreen oil aroma in the tea. Demand for teas which have this characteristic caused by natural wintergreen oil (Methyl Salicylate) in the leaves has led some unscrupulous estates to add the oil, which is used in various muscle rub products, to tea while processing. So buyers beware, if an Uva tea tastes too minty or menthol-like it has been artificially scented.

2 cup teapot 350 ml/5 oz. water at 90 °C/195 °F, 6 g tea – 2 minutes

FLAVOUR CHART

The relationship between a tea's colour and flavour is indicative rather than absolute. Nevertheless this chart can give you an idea of which type or colour of tea you might prefer. For those that enjoy light white flower aromas, try Taiwanese green oolongs and jasmine tea and for deeper floral scents Oriental Beauty and certain Wuyi Oolongs. People who love flavours similar to the fresh green flavours you find in spring vegetables are likely to enjoy sencha and some very lightly oxidized High Mountain Oolongs. Aromatic First Flush Darjeeling teas can combine fruity, floral and vegetal flavours. For delicate pome fruit flavours like pear and

Fruits POME/CITRUS/TROPICAL

Vegetal

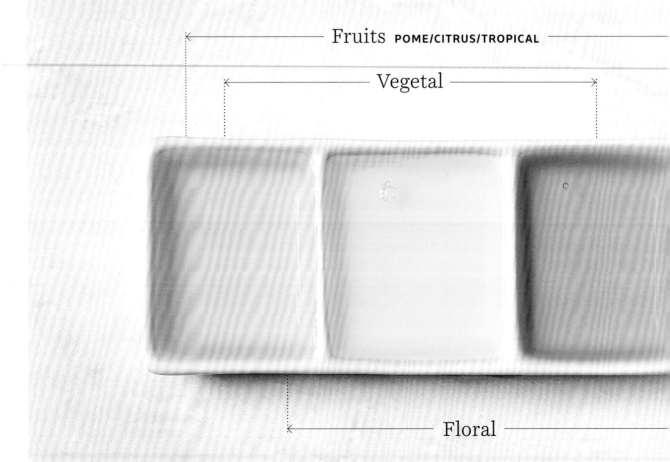

Floral

apple, high-quality Silver Needle teas may be a good choice. Many Phoenix Oolongs have distinctive tropical flavours like lychee, mango or pineapple while Oriental Beauty Oolongs as well as Second Flush Darjeeling can have a grape-like taste. Wuyi Oolongs are known for their peach and apricot aromas. If you like dark plums, well-made Shu Puerh teas can have this characteristic. For a fruity malty flavour, a Second Flush Assam or a Keemun black tea would be recommended. Finally for woody flavours, Hojicha gives a light smoky twig-like taste and many aged Sheng Puerh and some Shu Puerh can have a deep woody flavour.

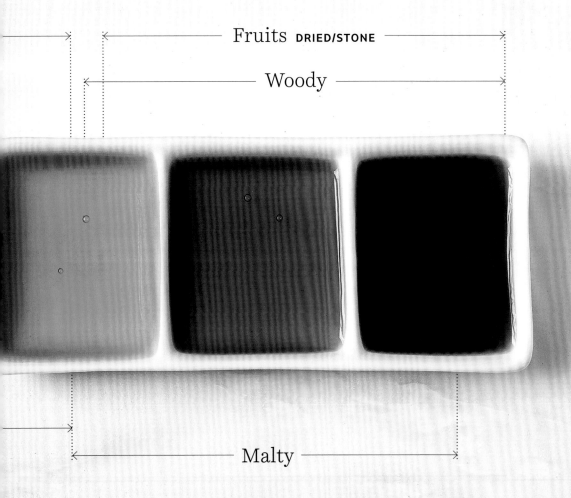

Fruits DRIED/STONE

Woody

Malty

FAMOUS BLENDS & HOME BLENDING

The English are famous throughout the world for their black tea blends. Sadly many of them are blended for economy today rather than quality so when buying be careful that you are getting what you want. The aim of a good blend is to offer something hard to achieve in a single origin single lot tea by combining the best qualities of several teas. The other aim is to offer consistency, a tea that changes remarkably little from season to season.

English Breakfast, Earl Grey and Russian Caravan are some of the best-known and most-loved blends. Here are some things to look for when choosing these blends as well as some alternative blend recipes you can make yourself. Considering the potential difference between the teas you will use as well as water will mean that over time you should tweak my suggested blends to your own taste.

ENGLISH BREAKFAST

English Breakfast is the king of breakfast blends and should be a rich black tea blend that works well with milk. Nowadays many English Breakfast blends have teas from unexpected origins. For example one leading English brand has a high percentage of tea from South America – not a place you'd expect your tea to come from. The blend probably originated in America and the name seems to have been around since the 19th century when the blend would have contained a high percentage of black tea from China.

HOME BREAKFAST

Many blends were originally made at home in the blending bowl found in large Victorian tea caddies which also had space for several teas. For all home blending I recommend using a big kitchen mixing bowl and some scales. For this blend you could also use a good African tea from Kenya or Malawi. For something sweeter, lighter and more aromatic I sometimes add a small percentage of Oriental Beauty oolong to the blend below.

33% Keemun
33% Second Flush Assam
33% Ceylon low-grown Sri Lankan tea

EARL GREY

Earl Grey's origins has been much debated and most of the mythology seems to involve a Chinese statesman giving the 19th-century British Prime Minister Earl Grey a secret formula for the tea. While the Chinese do fragrance their teas with flowers and even make a tea which is stuffed into a hollowed-out mandarin orange, they do not have bergamot fruit. Maybe Earl Grey was given something similar to Chinese mandarin orange tea and then when he tried to recreate it with something from another citrus fruit, he used bergamot oil. Bergamot are grown in the south of Italy and, by the mid-19th century when Earl Grey was probably invented, its oil was a popular perfume. Today pure bergamot oil is rarely used, instead most tea blenders use natural or artificial flavourings. Even when bergamot oil is listed in the ingredients, it is thought that many of these oils have been cut with lemon or orange oil to save money so slowly people are losing their taste for the real thing. If you cannot find a real bergamot Earl Grey you like, try the alternative overleaf.

LEMON PEKOE

This is almost not a blend as it is so simple. Before I made a blend of the same name with an Italian lemon oil for my shop, this was a blend I played around with and enjoyed. In my recipe I use a Second Flush Darjeeling tea but you could use another aromatic black tea if you prefer. When you blend this tea keep the whole lemon verbena leaves intact but before brewing the tea, the lemon verbena leaves should be crushed in your fingers to release the maximum flavour from them. Second Flush Darjeeling is a good tea to blend with the lemon verbena as its aromatics can match the herb but if you want more body and colour why not try blending in a stronger black tea as well.

90% Second Flush Darjeeling
10% Whole Lemon Verbena leaf herbal tea

RUSSIAN CARAVAN

While most Chinese teas came to the West came by ship, Russians originally received almost all their teas by land via camel caravans that transported the tea through Mongolia. The legend has it that the camp fires on the nightly stops imparted a gentle smoky taste to the tea. Today many Russian Caravan teas do not have much Chinese black tea in them but look out for those with Keemun, Yunnan, some Oolong and a little Lapsang as they are closer to the original.

JAPANESE CARAVAN

The Japanese love roasted tea and it occurred to me that you could make a flavoursome tea by blending black tea with Hojicha rather than Lapsang. If you choose a medium to strong bodied small-leafed *Camellia sinensis assamica* tea from India, Sri Lanka or Africa as your base, this should be a very satisfying but inexpensive blend. The percentage for each tea will vary a lot depending on how roasted the hojicha is, so do blend up small amounts first before settling on your own personal recipe.

70% Strong black tea
30% Hojicha

2
EASY LEAF BREWING

Shoving a tea bag in a cup and pouring hot water on it is no more making tea than putting a ready meal into a microwave is cooking. The great news is that to make an amazing cup of leaf tea takes the same amount of time and skill as making a mediocre cup of tea with a tea bag.

Using techniques or tools like the hoop tea scoop and hoop jug which can help you get the volume of leaf tea and also the temperature water right, making a delicious cup of tea every time is easy. Never forget that you are uniquely qualified to make the best cup of tea for yourself as you know what you like and what you want. The purpose of showing all these ways of brewing is to give you different styles to suit different teas as well as increasing your repertoire of tea-making methods. Imagine how boring your culinary life would be if you limited yourself just to one form of cooking or one type of ingredient – with tea, there are so many teas to choose from and so many ways to make them. Over time I hope you will improvise and create your own recipes and methods of making tea. Tea has a long history and its preparation has continually changed so let's hope we can all be part of this exciting period when tea is changing and starting to be appreciated in new and delicious ways.

TWIN TEAPOT METHOD

The twin teapot method is best for most black teas that require very hot water to make the most delicious aromatic cup of tea, such as Second Flush Darjeeling, Keemun and Lapsang teas. For this method you will need two teapots, one for brewing and another for serving.

Both teapots should be warmed before brewing the tea for two reasons; first to make sure that the water you pour in to brew the tea is not immediately cooled by a cold pot and secondly to make sure that the pot remains warm, which in turn will keep the tea warmer too. For the teapot you will serve in, it is best to put the lid back on to keep the pot as warm as it can be.

One of the main advantages of the twin teapot method is that the infusion is of equal strength so all the cups you pour will taste the same and you do not need to worry about pouring out the tea equally from a pot into different cups. Another bonus of this method is that the tea left in the pot can be covered in a tea cosy, kept warm and enjoyed later.

Method

Boil the kettle and fill both teapots at least half full. Refill the kettle with fresh cold water and boil again. Holding each of the teapots by the handle and spout, swirl the hot water around the pot to ensure it is warmed all over.

Pour away the hot water from the teapot you want to brew the tea in. Add the tea leaves for the number of cups you wish to brew.

When the kettle has boiled, pour the water into the brewing teapot, directing the water so that it swirls the leaves around the pot in a whirlpool-like action. Once you have finished pouring the water it is important to replace the lid while the leaves open and their full flavour and aroma are achieved.

Pour away the hot water from the second pot, this is your serving pot. When the tea has brewed to your preferred strength, pour it into the serving pot.

Make sure that you get every last drop of tea off the leaves because the last drops are often the most intensely flavoured and if the leaves are left without any liquid tea on them, they may be used again. A guide to determine whether they can be brewed again is to smell the leaves and if there is still a clear distinct aroma, a good second infusion is a possibility.

For the twin teapot method, using two teapots of a similar size yields the best results (right).

COOLING CUP METHOD

For black teas that work well with lower water temperatures, such as First Flush Darjeeling and even Assams and low grown *Camellia sinensis assamica* tea such as teas from Kenya and Malawi, I would recommend the following cooling cup method.

Cooling cup method for Assam type teas

Draw fresh cold water, boil it and wait until the water has stopped bubbling before pouring the hot water into the tea cups you will use. Make sure you add a tiny bit more water than you want to drink as the dried tea leaves will absorb a little of the liquid.

Add the correct amount of tea leaves to the pot and then carefully pour the water from the cups into the teapot and brew. When the tea has reached the desired strength, pour the tea back into the cups and serve.

Cooling cup method for First Flush Darjeeling

Draw fresh cold water, boil it and wait until the water has stopped bubbling before pouring the hot water into the teapot.

Pour the hot water from the pot into the tea cups you will use. Make sure you add a tiny bit more water than you want to drink as the dried tea leaves will absorb a little of the liquid. Empty any remaining water out of the teapot.

Add the correct amount of First Flush Darjeeling to the pot and then carefully pour the cooled water from the cups back into the teapot and brew. When the tea has reached the desired strength, pour the tea into the cups and serve.

One bonus with this style of brewing is that you know that the quantity of tea brewed will precisely fill the cups and there will be no tea left on the leaves so if you want to make a second or third infusion you can. If you like your First Flush brewed at an even lower temperature you can first pour the water from the kettle to the cups, then the pot, back to the cups and then finally into the pot with the tea leaves.

For safety's sake, remember to bring the teapot to the kettle, not the kettle to the teapot, when following this method (left).

MODERN GONG FU CHA

Gong fu cha translated from the Chinese means making tea with skill. It also refers to a style of tea making that has developed over centuries in China. The southern city of Chaozhou is particularly famed for its version of gong fu cha which can still be widely seen on its streets and in its houses. There they use a small local teapot or a Yixing teapot, three cups on a tea table or bowl, and a kettle heated over a brazier filled with olive stone charcoal.

A similar form of tea making was brought to Japan by Chinese monks who started Manpuku-ji Zen temple in the famous tea city of Uji south of Kyoto. Over 300 years later and the sencha tea ceremony schools continue to teach this style of tea. In more recent times, the Taiwanese have added the fairness jug and aroma cups to the equipment list that people may use. What started as a practical simple way of making tea has become in some circles an elaborate spectacle and display.

The modern gong fu cha method I am detailing is the simple style I use. It is not authentic or original, just a good way to brew East Asian teas to the similar concentration they are enjoyed in the areas they come from. It is also the one of the best ways to brew teas which are capable of being brewed many times. The method centres on a small brewing vessel which could be a teapot, a gaiwan or another infuser of between 100–150 ml/3½–5 oz. The size of the teapot is important as the small size corresponds to the small infusion you will make and also because a smaller brewing vessel is easier to use and quicker to pour than a larger one.

A fairness jug is essential as it can be used to cool water for green teas as well as serving or sharing tea amongst the drinkers. Of course if you are making and drinking tea for just yourself, feel free to pour directly into a larger cup unless you enjoy savouring the infusion from a smaller cup as many people like to do.

Method using a 150 ml/5 oz. brewer and 150 ml/5 oz. water

Wash any tightly rolled Oolong teas or pressed teas like Puerh with just-off-the-boil water for about 20–30 seconds and then ideally leave for the leaves to slowly open up.

Pour the water on to the leaves and replace the lid on the brewer. Some people like to stir the leaves with the brewer's lid and I have enjoyed some green teas made this way.

Carefully pour every last drop of tea off the leaves into the fairness jug so you get the best infusion and keep the leaves in good condition for the next infusion.

If you feel some of the brewing suggestions make too strong a tea for you, feel free to use less tea or lower the temperature of the water but the amounts of tea and the water temperature are similar to the way they are brewed in the areas the teas are made.

Fairness jug, an infuser and three serving cups (right, clockwise from top).

DOUBLE BREW

Double brew sounds like a strong beer but is an idea to make a single serving of tea in a portable vessel better. Tea drunk from paper cups and even thermos cups is often so insipid and uninspiring that a coffee can seem like a good choice. The idea for double brew came from a Ming dynasty leaf tea brewing method where a teapot was filled with water and then tea leaves were added to the water in the pot. The tea is then infused for the period of three breathes, poured into cups and then poured back into the pot to be reinfused for another three breathes.

The updated method gives intensity and complexity as you get infusions at different temperatures that highlight different qualities of the tea. It also partially solves the problem of one time infusions of multi-infusion teas like oolongs – you can use less tea than a one time infusion as with the two infusions you are extracting more. The process of transferring tea from one vessel to another lowers the tea temperature to a level which makes it more suited to drinking. No more burnt tongues!

Method

Draw fresh cold water and start boiling it.

Using a little less tea than suggested for the other methods, scoop out the tea and put it in the pot. Wait until the water has stopped bubbling before pouring the hot water into the pot. Infuse the tea for three long breathes or about 30 seconds before pouring the tea into the cup. Next, carefully pour back the liquid tea from the cup into the pot and infuse for another three breathes or about 30 seconds before pouring out ready to serve.

An infuser for the double brew method and a reusable glass travel cup (left).

FLOW BREWING

While I am believer in many traditional forms of tea, I am also attracted to innovations in both processing and brewing tea. Flow brewing, which adds layers of taste and complexity by brewing one tea through another, is one such innovation.

The idea for flow brewing came about one day at my shop when I was making a second infusion of a high grown Taiwanese oolong. Looking in front of me I saw another previously brewed tea in a pot and wondered what would happen if I poured the infusion of the oolong into the other tea, a Sri Lankan black tea. The resulting infusion was far more pleasing than I had imagined and it started my curiosity about other possible combinations.

The advantage of flow brewing is that you can use teas that would not work together as a blend because of a difference in brewing temperatures or leaf shapes. Another potential plus point of this technique is that unlike just mixing the teas, the teas seemed to work together to produce something unique and different from the sum of their parts. Often the resulting tea has an intense aroma and a much longer aftertaste.

Here are some basic guidelines to follow: Think about the temperature of the water with each tea and try to brew the teas according. For example, as a Second Flush Darjeeling responds better to hotter water you would infuse that before a First Flush. With certain combinations you may want to pour from one pot into a cup to cool it more before pouring the infusion into the next pot. As you are essentially brewing twice, neither the first nor the second infusion should be brewed too strong or the tea in the cup will become unpalatable. One way of judging the correct strength of the tea is to taste the tea as it is brewing. Of course this may be impossible with a tea brewed at a very high temperature but it is helpful for teas brewed at lower temperatures until you get your personal brewing formula fixed.

Some suggestions

Darjeeling Second Flush > Darjeeling First Flush

Formosa Oolong > Second Flush Assam

Darjeeling Second Flush > Jasmine

High Mountain Oolong > Assam or Darjeeling

High Grown Sri Lankan tea > Low Grown Sri Lankan tea

Earl Grey > Genmaicha

Jasmine > Sencha

Have fun inventing names for the above tea combinations!

Two infusers and a cup are all you need to try Flow Brewing (right).

CHAI

Aside from the exceptional leaf teas I drink on trips to India, the tea I look forward to trying the most is chai. In Kolkata, one of world's great tea-trading cities where chai is known as cha, it is often served in wonderful hand-thrown terracotta cups which seem to add an earthy sweet taste to the tea. In other areas conical recycled glasses are used to serve chai, often one within another to protect your hands from the piping hot frothy drink. The chaiwallahs who make these concoctions on street corners across the country are often famous for their special recipes. Below is a simple chai blend recipe you can personalize yourself and some simple instructions for making chai the easy way.

Chai Blend

Across India, there are regional difference in chai recipes. This recipe is based on a chai from the north-east of India but feel free to add small amounts of other herbs and spices, such as star anise, fennel seeds, peppercorns, nutmeg and bay leaves.

50 g/1¾ oz. Orthodox Assam
20 g/¾ oz. cardamom
10 g cinnamon
18.5 g dried sliced ginger
1.5 g cloves

Makes 100 g/3 oz.

If possible use a fuller fat milk like the buffalo milk often used to make chai in India as it will give the drink a lovely richness that a skimmed milk cannot. In India good CTC (the very small curled leaf tea) black tea is usually used and it is fine for a chai blend. My personal preference is always for a strong Orthodox tippy Assam. You may want to gently crush the spices before making the chai to release more of their flavour. My method of brewing chai is to use the cups you will drink from to measure the amount of milk (approximately 2 cups) you will use. By gently warming the milk and making sure not to scald it by going over 70°C/158°F, you should be able to make a naturally sweet drink but if you enjoy your chai very sweet do feel free to add sugar at the end.

14–16 g Chai tea
340 ml/11½ oz. whole milk

Makes 2 servings

Pour the milk into a saucepan. Alternatively you can measure how much you will need by using the two cups or glasses you will drink from.

Gently warm the milk on a low heat for 2–2½ minutes. Add the chai tea and slowly stir the milk and tea in the saucepan.

Keep the milk at a temperature of between 55°C–60°C/130°F–140°F while the chai brews. You may have to occasionally remove the saucepan from the stove to keep the milk within these temperatures.

Taste the tea with a spoon to check how it is brewing and when it has reached your desired strength, remove the saucepan from the stove and pour the chai into your two cups or glasses.

PUERH TEA THE PRESSED AGED TEA

Puerh is the most unusual category of tea, one which improves with age and can increase in value over time. It comes from Yunnan province in the far south-west of China and is named after the town where the tea was often traded. There are two types, raw (Sheng) Puerh or cooked (Shu) Puerh and both are usually pressed and sold as discus-like cakes called bings or bricks rather than loose leaf.

Once, all Puerh tea was the raw Sheng variety which starts off as an astringent green-like tea that oxidizes and undergoes some microbial changes over years to became a rich smooth dark tea. As this process can take up to a decade or more, supply could not meet demand in Puerh-loving cities like Hong Kong in the 1970s so some bright spark in Yunnan's capital city Kunming invented the Shu process that fast-ages the tea. This is done by piling up the processed tea leaves and keeping them moist and warm for over a month so changes that mimic the taste of aged Sheng Puerh happen. The resulting teas are often served with dim sum dumplings in Chinese restaurants around the world and can be delicious but watch out for badly processed ones that taste mouldy or fishy. As Shu Puerh has already undergone a transformation, older Shu Puerhs often taste similar to younger versions of the same tea, so unlike Sheng Puerhs there is not a large market for vintage Shu Puerh.

Aged Sheng Puerh tea is drunk not just for the taste but for the feeling of energy it can give. Puerh connoisseurs often look for tea made from old trees as it usually has more depth and can have stronger energy than tea from normal tea plantation fields. As the tea can be aged and drunk for decades, comes with date of production and information about the tea trees, and often a precise geographical area, an investment market not unlike the wine market in the West has developed in Asia. Like wine, where and how the tea has been stored is also very important with the humidity and changes of temperature from season to season playing a large part in how the tea develops. Before buying expensive Puerh, it is best to order and taste a range of samples. Then you can see if Puerh will be a big part of your tea life. It is the kind of tea that is not for everyone but, for those who love it, Puerh can quickly become an obsession and the only tea they drink.

Drinking younger Sheng Puerh has become more popular as older Sheng Puerh has become expensive and rare. Traditionally these unaged green tea-like teas were considered to be too strong or harsh for many people's palates in the traditional Puerh drinking communities. As with other teas, there is a huge spectrum of quality and flavour, and there are some recent Puerhs I can enjoy drinking and some I do not. With the ones I like, I often brew them hot and then use the same leaves to do a delicious cold brew – one of my favourite brands produces a Puerh that, especially when young, has a pronounced apricot taste when cold infused overnight. One friend from Yunnan also taught me a way of making those teas that are a little too astringent and green for my taste more palatable. She recommends roasting the small amount of tea leaves you will use in a frying pan for a few minutes on a low-medium heat before brewing.

A stone pressed Sheng Puerh cake made on Mengsong mountain, southern Yunnan, China (left).

HOW TO CAREFULLY BREAK UP A PUERH CAKE OR BRICK

A puerh knife, a letter opener or a blunt pen knife are perfect for helping to break up a cake or brick. Put the cake or brick flat on a surface, carefully insert the knife into the edge of the cake or brick and give it a gentle jiggle. Repeat this action around the edge of the cake or brick until you can either separate the cake into two halves or into various layers of the tea. With stone-pressed Puerhs you can usually separate the remaining leaves using just your fingers but with machine-pressed Puerhs often you will need the knife again to prise off the leaves intact and whole. Often I do not try to break up every small slab of tea as when you wash the tea with hot water from the kettle before brewing, the leaves will also come apart. Having washed the leaves and poured off all the water I sometimes even carefully separate any leaves still clumped together with my fingers before brewing.

For everyday drinking Puerhs that you intend to drink quickly and come in really tightly pressed cakes and bricks which cannot be easily taken apart with a knife, steaming is an option. Place the brick or cake in a steamer or a colander over a pan of simmering water for 5 minutes on a low heat, rest for a couple of minutes then try to gently break up the tea. If it is still not easy to break up the tea, steam for another 5 minutes and try again until it can be easily broken up. Puerh tea is best made using the gong fu method.

Making Shu Puerh

Wash 6 g of tea with boiling water for about 20–30 seconds and pour off the liquid. Do this again and then infuse the tea with 150 ml/5 oz. of boiling water for 20 seconds before decanting the tea into a fairness jug. Subsequent infusions will be about 30 seconds long until the tea loses its potency when longer infusions may be needed.

Making Young Sheng Puerh

Wash 6 g of tea with 95°C/200°F water for about 20–30 seconds and pour off the liquid. Next infuse the tea with 150 ml/5 oz. of water at 95°C/200°F for 15-20 seconds before decanting the tea into a fairness jug. Subsequent infusions will also be about 15–20 seconds long until the tea loses its potency when longer infusions may be necessary.

Making Aged Sheng Puerh

Wash 6 g of tea with boiling water for about 20-30 seconds at least once. If the tea has a lot of storage taste it may require two washes. Then infuse the tea with 150 ml/5 oz. of boiling water for 20 seconds before decanting the tea into a fairness jug. Subsequent infusions will also be about 20 seconds long until the tea loses its potency when longer infusions may be needed.

Quo Vadis

I suspect everyone who knows Jeremy Lee can remember when they first met him. He has such a big personality and is such a great cook that it is impossible to forget him or his fabulous food once you have encountered them. The first time we met was at a Slow Food festival ten years ago where I was brewing up some cold brew Darjeeling tea and we have been friends ever since. When Jeremy joined the Hart brothers at Quo Vadis and we started supplying the restaurant and club I was thrilled because Quo Vadis is one of the few places left that captures Soho's spirit and atmosphere. It has been a restaurant since 1926 and the building is also famous for being where Karl Marx lived and wrote much of *Das Kapital*.

Sometimes friends take me to afternoon tea at one of the posh London hotels. Of course some of the venues are fabulous but often they seem expensive for what they offer and their cakes not very traditional – I do not expect to find macaroons or cupcakes with their sickly sweet frosting on an afternoon tea menu in England. So when I have foreign friends visiting London and I want to show them how good British food can be, I like taking them to have a late lunch/afternoon tea at Quo Vadis. I recommend starting with Jeremy's legendary hot smoked eel sandwich with its very moreish horseradish sauce. For some other classics maybe try sharing some of those delicious cheesy filo pastry-wrapped salsify (a lovely local root vegetable) or kickshaws (mini deep fried meat or fish pies first mentioned in English by Shakespeare in Henry IV Part II says *The Oxford English Dictionary*).

Next comes the beautifully illustrated Pudding menu which asks you the question 'Fancy Tea? Lots to choose from. Just ask.' Once you have decided on a tea, time to choose one or more of the traditional favourites, and you cannot really go wrong – from sticky puddings to tarts and cakes often accompanied by creams and custards – there is something for every mood and it changes seasonally so you should visit at least four times a year. Much as I adore sitting in the dining room with its pretty stained-glass windows, if it is summer why not ask if you can take your tea and cake to one of the outside tables and become part of Soho street life.

This page, clockwise from top: Quo Vadis tea caddies, chrome door plates in the shape of the restaurant's iconic art deco sign, the dining room filled with wild flowers and artwork by John Broadley who illustrates the menus, and a pot of tea, a cake and some shortcake biscuits. Left: The outside seats of Quo Vadis are a delight in good weather.

The stained glass windows of the dining room at Quo Vadis provide a fleeting glimpse of Soho's colourful street life outside.

3
LOWER TEMPERATURE TEAS

Cold tea sounds a bit like an insult or a punishment, especially to those who come from countries where they drink their tea piping hot. Nevertheless, around the world chilled iced teas are becoming more and more popular. Mostly these teas come in cans and bottles and can be found in chiller cabinets across America, Asia and Europe. In Japan, for example, about half the tea grown now goes into ready-to-drink teas and many of these teas will be refrigerated and served chilled.

My interest and involvement with lower temperature tea is long standing, primarily because I view homemade tea as the most delicious alternative to soft drinks. While most of us enjoy the occasional soft drink, it is becoming obvious that soft drinks production and consumption on today's scale has major environmental and public health issues. When I was a kid, soft drinks came in returnable bottles, today they come in one-time-use throwaway containers. Water extraction for production, the transportation and refrigeration of soft drinks are other problems. Both sugary and 'sugar-free' diet drinks with artificial sweeteners have been linked to obesity and ingredients found in some soft drinks have been linked to serious diseases. Homemade tea is not only healthy but usually inexpensive and very easy to make.

Ambient, cold brew and tea sodas are lower temperature teas designed to suit different occasions and moods. Ambient tea is best when combined with food or when you want to enjoy a very special tea in a way other than a hot infusion. Cold brew is great when you want something really cold and refreshing to drink, while tea soda is essentially a delicious soft drink with fizz but no sugar that can be prepared very quickly with normal kitchen ingredients, including tea.

AMBIENT TEA TEA FOR FINE FOOD

The main types of tea (green, oolong, black and aged) produce a huge variety of floral, fruity, vegetal and woody flavours capable of complementing numerous foods. Many foods are also thought to have tea flavours so the potential for pairing the two seems obvious. Tea may even be a better match than wine for some notoriously difficult food pairings like asparagus, artichokes, chocolate and spicy foods. If tea can be successfully paired with many foods and with a demand for complex non-alcoholic drinks, why isn't tea more often paired with fine food?

In Asia, where tea originates, everyday tea is often drunk with foods that were originally street foods, such as sushi and dim sum, but fine tea is not usually drunk with fine foods. Alcohol is the traditional accompaniment of a Chinese banquet and even the formal meal within a full-length Japanese tea ceremony.

In the West, with the exception of the afternoon tea experience, hot drinks are not usually served through a meal but only offered at the end of a meal when both tea and coffee are seen as good digestives with a pleasant astringency to counteract the sweetness of the dessert course. The drinks we enjoy during a meal are almost always served chilled or at room temperature.

Faced with these issues I started exploring a new way of serving tea in a fine dining context. Unlike traditional hot brews (a few minutes at temperatures above 65°C/150°F) or cold brews (many hours between 1–5°C/33–40°F), ambient brewing is done for usually less than an hour with water at cool ambient temperatures between 10–20°C/50–68°F, and served within those temperatures. Ambient brewing is a happy medium: it quickly yields a brewed tea that has more flavour, body, structure and aroma than cold-brewed tea, while avoiding the astringency that hot brewing processes can create.

Ambient tea also feels appropriate for service with fine food as it can be poured from a bottle or decanter into glasses at a temperature that creates no condensation and is pleasant to hold in your hands as you admire the tea's colour. As the ambient tea warms up the aromas and structure will change, just like a wine, but the changes are subtle compared to the dramatic changes with hot and cold brew tea, making ambient tea a much more reliable partner for fine food. Ambient tea debuted at the RAW Natural Wine Festival in 2016 and then working with Fera at Claridge's we worked to match many teas with their Michelin-starred food.

Gyokuro

Gyokuro pairs wonderfully with both cooked and raw fish as well as a variety of vegetables.

12 g Gyokuro
750 ml/25 oz. room temperature water

Makes 4–5 servings

Put the leaves in a jug/pitcher or decanter. Fill up the vessel with the water and brew for 40 minutes.

Taste the tea, remembering that the top of the tea is likely to be lighter than the bottom part of the infusion. If it isn't quite ready continue to taste every 10 minutes. When ready to serve, strain and decant the tea into a bottle or decanter. Serve in a wine glass.

Roasted Black Tea

Roasted black tea is a rarity but we hope there will more available in the future. Black Sun, a Japanese black tea we roast in London, pairs well with pork, smoked and oily fish as well as chocolate desserts.

12 g roasted black tea
750 ml/25 oz. room temperature
water

Makes 4–5 servings

Put the leaves in a jug/pitcher or decanter. Fill up the vessel with the water and brew for 40 minutes.

Taste the tea, remembering that the top of the tea is likely to be lighter than the bottom part of the infusion. If it isn't quite ready continue to taste the tea every 10 minutes. When it's ready to serve, strain and decant the tea into a bottle or decanter. Serve in a wine glass.

First Flush Darjeeling

First Flush Darjeeling works well with fish, white meats and salads. It will also pair with white cheese or dishes made with cream.

12 g First Flush Darjeeling
750 ml/25 oz. room temperature water

Makes 4–5 servings

Put the leaves in a jug/pitcher or decanter. Fill up the vessel with the water and brew for 40 minutes.

Taste the tea, remembering that the top of the tea is likely to be lighter than the bottom part of the infusion. If it isn't quite ready continue to taste the tea every 10 minutes. When it's ready to serve, strain and decant the tea into a bottle or decanter. Serve in a wine glass.

Oriental Beauty

Oriental Beauty is well suited to shellfish and crustaceans, as well as dark green vegetables including asparagus.

12 g Oriental Beauty
750 ml/25 oz. room temperature water

Makes 4–5 servings

Put the leaves in a jug/pitcher or decanter. Fill up the vessel with the water and brew for 40 minutes.

Taste the tea, remembering that the top of the tea is likely to be lighter than the bottom part of the infusion. If it isn't quite ready continue to taste the tea every 10 minutes. When it's ready to serve, strain and decant the tea into a bottle or decanter. Serve in a wine glass.

Shu Puerh

A strongly-brewed Shu Puerh is capable of working well with beef and other red meats as well as mushrooms and truffles.

12 g Shu Puerh
750 ml/25 oz. room temperature water

Makes 4–5 servings

Put the leaves in a jug/pitcher or decanter. Fill up the vessel with the water and brew for 40 minutes.

Taste the tea, remembering that the top of the tea is likely to be lighter than the bottom part of the infusion. If it isn't quite ready continue to taste the tea every 10 minutes. When it's ready to serve, strain and decant the tea into a bottle or decanter. Serve in a wine glass.

Fera at Claridge's

I find grand restaurants intimidating and grand restaurants in grand hotels even more so. It seems difficult to fully relax and enjoy what should be a very special time with friends or family. Fera has changed the way I feel about grand hotel restaurants with its warm service, opulent but relaxed setting and its exquisite food. Of course I am biased because I have worked with the great team there for several years but many visitors' experiences have been similar to mine.

The team's attention to detail is incredible. They attended many tasting sessions before they decided on their selection of teas and they commissioned a range of unique handmade tea ware and utensils for their hot tea service. Likewise, when we collaborated with Fera for a series of seven-course dinners paired with Ambient tea, we did several tastings with Raphaël, the restaurant director, and Dan, the chef, to select the most appropriate tea for every dish.

The seasonality of their dishes means that pairings may change but I can heartily recommend the pairing of fish like halibut with Taiwanese high mountain oolong and the roasted black tea Black Sun with some of the lighter meat dishes. The aim was never to cater just for teetotalers. Raphaël and I believe that the complexity and variety in tea and wine means each can complement different dishes throughout a meal, keeping the palette and mind fresh to more fully appreciate the food as well as what you are drinking.

As well as the restaurant's grand main room, Fera has some other special places. First, there is a tiny five-seat bar where you can enjoy exceptional cocktails made with local gins, some great wines or maybe an after-dinner digestif or tea. Secondly, if you ask them politely you are likely to be given a brief tour of their kitchen to see the skillful chefs preparing your food. You may be surprised by the calm and cool atmosphere of the kitchen which comes from their choice of cookers, a sophisticated cooling system and temperament of the team. And finally there is Aulis, the six-seat development kitchen. Aulis, which you enter through the kitchen, is a bit like going to a very exclusive Japanese restaurant with a short counter and a chef who serves up many small courses with the freshest, most unusual ingredients. Fera is a restaurant where many different culinary experiences are possible and one where they make a huge effort to show how well tea can work with fine food.

This page, clockwise from top: The side entrance to Claridge's hotel and Fera, ambient tea in a double-walled glass decanter, meticulous preparation of a dish in the kitchen, two glasses of ambient tea. Opposite page: A tea and food pairing at Aulis, Fera's six-seat development kitchen.

staurant director
Rodriguez carries
ambient tea
the historic
dining room.

COLD BREW FOR ADULTS, KIDS + HOT SUMMERS

Cold infusing tea is a refreshing way to enjoy leaf tea in summers. I learnt about the method when I lived in Asia in the 1990s. Asian summers can be unpleasantly hot and humid so cold brew teas were an important part of my daily life. As well as using new tea leaves, I often use leaves I have previously made hot infusions from. As I usually just use mains water, cold brew teas represent not only amazing value but also they are pretty environmentally friendly when compared to soft drinks which have been transported many miles from the factory, refrigerated for a long time before use and packed in one-time-use containers.

Cold brew teas are a great way to get kids involved in leaf tea as most teas can be prepared safely without hot water. Hopefully cold brewing tea also introduces them to lots of different teas so they can find out what they most enjoy. As cold brew teas are less astringent than hot brewed teas, they suit many children who have developed a sweet tooth, but of course cold brews have none of the sugars or additives found in many soft drinks. My daughter loves making birthday blends of tea to give to friends and cold brew blends are an easy way to start experimenting with simple blends. Hopefully sharing cold brewing with your kids is the beginning of a great tea adventure for them and the start of one of the healthiest habits anyone can have.

Sparkling cold brew recipes are perfect for parties. They make a really vibrant non-alcoholic fizz which make anyone who cannot drink alcohol feel part of a special party and the celebration. Of all my tea brewing ideas, this has probably been the most successful. I am always thrilled to hear when someone has picked up the method from a magazine article, book or tasting I have done and then they have incorporated into their tea-making rituals. Of course you could cold brew a tea and then carbonate it with a machine but I tend to prefer low tech solutions and have found the taste of sparkling cold brew to be better.

Sparkling First Flush Darjeeling

12 g First Flush Darjeeling (AV-2 clonal First Flush teas are often most fragrant with tropical fruit flavours)
750 ml/25 oz. bottle sparkling mineral water (highly carbonated is best)

Makes 4–5 servings

Open the bottle of sparkling mineral water and gently pour out 50 ml/1¾ oz. of the water. Add the First Flush Darjeeling to the bottle using a paper or plastic funnel and screw the top back on. Store upright in a refrigerator for 3–4 hours.

Using a kitchen towel carefully and slowly open the bottle over a sink. When the infusion stops surging, pour through a fine mesh strainer directly into champagne glasses. The bottle top can be put on again temporarily but all the sparkling infusion should be served as swiftly as possible.

You can also cold brew this tea overnight with 8 g tea in 1 litre/33¾ oz. still water.

Sparkling Jasmine

12 g jasmine tea (you can use any jasmine but Jasmine Pearls are the easiest to put in the sparkling water bottle)
750 ml/25 oz. bottle sparkling mineral water

Makes 4–5 servings

Open the bottle of sparkling mineral water and gently pour out 50 ml/1¾ oz. of the water. Add the jasmine tea to the bottle using a paper or plastic funnel and screw the top back on. Store upright in the refrigerator for 3–4 hours.

Using a kitchen towel carefully and slowly open the bottle over a sink. When the infusion stops surging, pour through a fine mesh strainer directly into champagne glasses. The bottle top can be put on again temporarily but all the sparkling infusion should be served as swiftly as possible.

You can also cold brew this tea overnight with 8 g tea in 1 litre/33¾ oz. still water.

Darjeeling Second Flush

10 g Darjeeling Second Flush
1 litre/33¾ oz. water

Makes 6 servings

Put the Darjeeling Second Flush into a jug/pitcher and fill up the vessel with the water.

Put the jug/pitcher in the refrigerator and allow the tea to infuse overnight or for about 8 hours. Strain and serve.

Alternatively, use Oriental Beauty but add some extra strong black tea more for body and colour.

High Mountain Oolong

10 g High-grown Taiwanese Mountain Oolong
1 litre/33¾ oz. water

Makes 6 servings

Brew the tea with hot water at 95°C/200°F for about 20 seconds to help open up the ball rolled leaves.

Put the tea into a jug/pitcher and fill up the vessel with the water. Put the the jug/pitcher in the refrigerator and allow the tea to infuse overnight or for about 8 hours. Strain and serve. Alternatively try lower grown Taiwanese green oolong teas for a similarly sweet fragrant cold brew.

Sencha

8 g sencha
1 litre/33¾ oz. water

Makes 6 servings

Put the sencha into a jug/pitcher and fill up the vessel with the water.

Put the jug/pitcher in the refrigerator and allow the tea to infuse overnight or for about 8 hours. Strain and serve.

Alternatively, try a roasted Japanese tea, like hojicha. Use 8 g of hojicha and brew overnight for a dark bitter-sweet tea.

Lemon Verbena

4 g lemon verbena
1 litre/33¾ oz. water

Makes 6 servings

Put the lemon verbena leaves into a jug/pitcher. Briefly blanch with hot water and pour off all the liquid, leaving the leaves in the jug and then fill up the jug with the water.

Put the jug/pitcher in the refrigerator and allow the tea to infuse overnight or for about 8 hours. Strain and serve.

For another lemon-like herbal tea why not also try lemongrass.

TEA SODAS SPARKLING TEA SOFT DRINKS

Tea sodas are sugar-free sparkling soft drinks you make yourself with tea and other natural ingredients. Everything you need might be in your kitchen or can be found at any large supermarket or whole food store. Tea sodas are quick and fun to make and, like cold brews, kids love making them as well as drinking them.

The inspiration for tea sodas came from discovering cold brew tea in Asia. On one particular visit to Taiwan in the mid 1990s, after a formal gong fu tea tasting I was served a cold brew jasmine in a tall champagne glass which made me think about cold brewing the same tea in sparkling water.

After lots of testing and tasting I started a cold brew tea company in 2000 with lemon, jasmine and oolong tea blends developed to work in both still and sparkling water. The idea of sugar and artificial additive-free drinks has always been my goal so after coming up with the original tea recipes I wanted to develop homemade drinks with similar flavours to the most popular soft drinks. Obviously the fresh natural ingredients you will use are very different from the industrial flavourings used in soft drinks so these drinks can never replicate their tastes but you will find the Senchades and Kitchen Cola refreshing and very delicious in a new way.

If you are making and serving tea sodas for kids, why not pour them into labelled glass bottles to complete the soft drink experience. You can always wash the bottles and use them again and again (right).

Kitchen Cola

Trying to recreate a cola taste was very interesting. I realized that many soft drinks have lots of astringency and lots of sugar so added citrus for the citric astringency and vanilla to sweeten it without sugar. With this recipe the cola element comes from the cinnamon which combines with the tea and other ingredients to evoke the famous flavour. As our taste is so much guided by colour, it may feel a little strange to drink a light coloured clear cola but since the colourings used in certain colas have been linked to cancer, I hope you will agree that a lighter coloured cola is the better option.

If you really want to try and recreate a darker colour, you can try this quick cold brew method. Take 10 g of a strong brewing tea like an Assam, wash it with water at 90°C/195°F for about 10 seconds and pour off all the hot water. Next add 50 ml/1¾ oz. cold water and brew for 30–45 seconds. Pour off the brew into your cola and enjoy the warm brown colour as well as the taste. Feel free to add ice and garnish with a slice of lemon or lime.

2 g/⅓–½ **vanilla pod**
8 g **cinnamon bark, broken into bits**
3 g **Darjeeling Second Flush**
¼ **lime, cut into pieces**
330 ml/11 oz. or 500 ml/17 oz. **chilled sparkling water**

Makes 2–3 servings

Cut the vanilla pod down the middle and then cut into small bits. Put into an infuser basket or fillable tea bag with the cinnamon bark, tea and lime, and then put the basket or tea bag into the bottle you will use for infusing.

Gently pour the sparkling water over the tea, trying not to create too much fizz.

Put the lid on the infuser bottle and let infuse for 5 minutes.

Open and serve in a glass. If the infuser bottle is less than 500 ml/17 oz. you can re-infuse the tea with the rest of the water.

Lime Senchade

I love the clarity and refreshing buzz of the lime combined with sencha, but if you prefer lemonade do try your own recipes with a combination of lemon and a little lime. This drink reminds me a little of the lovely lime sodas you get from street stalls in India but the addition of the sencha adds something extra, smoother and more complex. As well as cooling you, it feels really good for you. Feel free to add ice and garnish with a slice of lime or maybe even some fresh mint.

1 g/¼ vanilla pod
4 g sencha
¼ lime, cut into pieces
330 ml/11 oz. or 500 ml/17 oz. chilled
  sparkling water

Makes 2–3 servings

Cut the vanilla pod down the middle and then cut into small bits. Put into the infuser basket or fillable tea bag with the tea and lime and then put the basket or tea bag into the bottle you will use for infusing.

Gently pour the sparkling water over the tea, trying not to create too much fizz. Put the lid on the infuser bottle and let infuse for 5 minutes.

Open and serve. If the infuser bottle is less than 500 ml/17 oz. you can re-infuse the tea with the rest of the water.

Pineapple Senchade

For a tropical taste, try a Pineapple Senchade with its gentle tang. You will need a sweet juicy pineapple so check to see if the fruit has a mild pineapple aroma at its base which is a good sign of ripeness. Being able to pluck leaves from the top of the fruit is no guarantee of sweetness but some swear by this test. For a garnish, a simple pineapple wedge or even a small sprig of mint is best because strong citrus fruits like lime and lemon would overwhelm the delicate pineapple aroma and taste.

1 g/¼ vanilla pod
4 g sencha
45–50 g/1½–2 oz. sweet juicy pineapple,
  cut into pieces
330 ml/11 oz. or 500 ml/17 oz. chilled
  sparkling water

Makes 2–3 servings

Cut the vanilla pod down the middle and then cut into small bits. Put into the infuser basket or fillable tea bag with the tea and pineapple and then put the basket or tea bag into the bottle you will use for infusing.

Gently pour the sparkling water over the tea, trying not to create too much fizz. Put the lid on the infuser bottle and let infuse for 5 minutes.

Open and serve. If the infuser bottle is less than 500 ml/17 oz. you can re-infuse the tea with the rest of the water.

Ginger Senchade

As well as enjoying this as a kind of Asian ginger ale, Ginger Senchade, like the Kitchen Cola and Lime Senchade, makes a great mixer for both alcoholic and non-alcoholic cocktails. What I like most about this drink is the way it combines the cooling element of lime and sencha with the heat and sweetness of grated ginger and vanilla. Like all the recipes, feel free to adjust the quantities. For those who really love a strong ginger kick 12 g of ginger might not be enough, whereas for others who want just a background taste of ginger 7 g or 8 g might be enough. Feel free to add ice and garnish with a slice of lemon or cucumber.

2 g/⅓–½ vanilla pod
12 g fresh ginger, grated
4 g sencha
⅛ lime, cut into pieces
330 ml/11 oz. or 500 ml/17 oz. chilled
   sparkling water

Makes 2–3 servings

Cut the vanilla pod down the middle and then cut into small bits. Put into the infuser basket or fillable tea bag with the ginger, tea and lime and then put the basket or tea bag into the bottle you will use for infusing.

Gently pour the sparkling water over the tea, trying not to create too much fizz. Put the lid on the infuser bottle and let infuse for 5 minutes.

Open and serve. If the infuser bottle is less than 500 ml/17 oz. you can re-infuse the tea with the rest of the water.

4

FRESH FRUIT TEA QUARTERS
TEA + FRUIT JUICE

Freshly pressed juice is so vital and delicious. On Sunday mornings I like making orange juice for my family with an old-fashioned squeezer. Much as I adore it I can't drink a lot of it and indeed without a large supply of oranges I cannot make more than a small glass each for the family. Maybe nature has long been trying to tell us what nutritionists are now all saying, that we should only consume a small amount of fruit juice as much of it has too many empty calories and not enough fibre. So it got me thinking about how could I combine two loves – tea and juice – to make something new and tasty that could be drunk in larger quantities without the fear of a sugar rush. An amazing meal at the restaurant The Clove Club where I was served a lavender-infused apple juice with hot oolong tea in a wine glass also influenced these delicious hybrid teas.

I came up with the name 'tea quarters' because the fruit juice the tea is infused in is diluted to a quarter of its original strength, which reduces the calories in most fruit juices from about 40 per 100 ml/3½ oz. to just 10. The possible combinations are endless and I believe you will be able to come up with some of your own personal favourites after a little experimentation.

In summer you can also made tasty tea popsicles by using the recipes for Fruit Ices and pouring the fresh fruit tea quarter into moulds and placing them in the freezer for a few hours or overnight. In winter hot fruit tea quarters are a great pick-me-up. When it's getting chilly outside or you feel like you are coming down with a cold, why not try a hot fresh fruit tea quarter to give yourself a mental and physical boost.

This is one of the few recipes in the book with no tea. If you really need the caffeine why not substitute the lemon verbena with 12 g of lemon oil fragranced tea. However I love the combination of these two tastes so much that I would recommend you try this recipe first.

Oranges and Lemon Verbena

5 g lemon verbena
250 ml/8½ oz. freshly-squeezed orange
juice, ideally without too much pulp
750 ml/25 oz. water

Makes 6 servings

Place the lemon verbena leaves in a 1 litre/ 33¾ oz. jug/pitcher or carafe. Briefly blanch the tea with hot water and pour off all the liquid, leaving the leaves in the jug/pitcher.

Add the orange juice, top up with the water and stir the infusion.

Put the jug/pitcher in the refrigerator and allow it to infuse overnight or for about 8 hours. Strain and serve for a tangy addictive drink.

Hot Oranges and Lemon Verbena

6–10 lemon verbena leaves
approx. 55 ml/2 oz. freshly-squeezed
orange juice

Makes 1 serving

Brew the lemon verbena leaves in a small 150 ml/5 oz. teapot with water at 90°C/195°F for about 1 minute.

Fill a quarter of a cup or mug with orange juice. Add the lemon verbena infusion and serve.

Do you like those brain-tingling citron pressés that you get in French cafés? If you do but want something smoother with a lovely green tea tang, Lemon Green Tea Quarters are well worth trying.

Lemon Green

freshly squeezed juice of 1–2 lemons
15 g sencha
approx. 920–960 ml/31–32 oz. water

Makes 6 servings

Pour the freshly squeezed lemon juice into a 1 litre/33¾ oz. jug/pitcher.

Add the sencha and top up the infusion with water.

Put the jug/pitcher in the refrigerator and allow it to infuse overnight or for about 8 hours. Strain and serve for a bracing breakfast drink.

Hot Lemon Green

3–4 g sencha
1 teaspoon freshly squeezed lemon juice

Makes 1 serving

Brew the sencha leaves in a small 150 ml/ 5 oz. teapot with water at 70°C/160°F for about 1 minute.

Pour the lemon juice into a cup or mug, add the tea and serve.

This combination was inspired by the brilliant beverage boys and girls at The Clove Club in London. Their very sophisticated version uses a herb infused apple juice and is served warm.

Apple Oolong

15 g green oolong
250 ml/8½ oz. freshly
pressed sweet apple juice
750 ml/25 oz. water

Makes 6 servings

Put the green oolong tea in a 1 litre/33¾ oz. jug/pitcher or carafe. Briefly brew/wash with hot water for 30 seconds to open the ball-rolled oolong and pour off all the liquid, leaving just the leaves in the jug/pitcher.

Add the sweet apple juice, top up with the water and stir the infusion.

Put the jug/pitcher in the refrigerator and allow it to infuse overnight or for about 8 hours. Strain and serve for a soothing aromatic drink.

Hot Apple Oolong

5 g green oolong
approx. 55 ml/2 oz. freshly
pressed sweet apple juice

Makes 1 serving

Put the green oolong in a small 150 ml/5 oz. teapot. Wash the green oolong leaves for 30 seconds with 95°C/200°F water to open up the leaves before brewing for about 1½ minutes in 90°C/195°F water.

Fill a quarter of a cup or mug with the apple juice. Pour the oolong tea into the mug with the apple juice. Many infusions are possible with this tea so keep on brewing.

Sweet and tart with a great zing is why pink grapefruit is one of my favourite fruit juices. The colour is also delightful and feels special no matter how often I drink it. Jasmine tea shares some of grapefruit's sweetness and pleasant astringency so they work well together.

Grapefruit Jasmine

12–15 g jasmine tea
250 ml/8½ oz. freshly pressed
   pink grapefruit juice
750 ml/25 oz. water

Makes 6 servings

Put the jasmine tea in a 1 litre/33¾ oz. jug/pitcher or carafe. Add the pink grapefruit juice, top up with the water and stir.

Put the jug/pitcher in the refrigerator and allow it to infuse overnight or for about 8 hours. Strain and serve for an invigorating drink.

Hot Grapefruit Jasmine

3 g jasmine tea
approx. 55 ml/2 oz. freshly pressed
   pink grapefruit juice

Makes 1 serving

Put the jasmine tea in a small 150 ml/5 oz. teapot. Brew with water at 80°C/175°F for about a minute.

Fill a quarter of a cup or mug with the pink grapefruit juice. Pour the jasmine tea into the cup and serve.

Modern transportation and retailing make enjoying watermelon in winter possible but somehow it does not feel right so save its delights for summer. The perfume and natural sweetness of Oriental Beauty tea adds aroma as well as some body to the watered-down watermelon juice. The hot version is a little more of an acquired taste but well worth a try.

Watermelon Oolong

15–20 g Oriental Beauty Oolong
250 ml/8½ oz. freshly pressed
watermelon juice
750 ml/25 oz. water

Makes 6 servings

Place the Oriental Beauty Oolong in a 1 litre/33¾ oz. jug/pitcher or carafe.

Add the watermelon juice, top up with the water and stir the infusion.

Put the vessel in the refrigerator and allow it to infuse overnight or for about 8 hours. Strain and serve for an invigorating drink.

Hot Watermelon Oolong

approx. 55 ml/2 oz. freshly pressed
watermelon juice
4 g Oriental Beauty Oolong

Makes 1 serving

Fill a quarter of a cup or mug with fresh watermelon juice.

Put the Oriental Beauty Oolong into a small 150 ml/5 oz. teapot Brew with water at 90°C/195°F for about a minute.

This is a tea which also works very well with the double brew method (see page 53).

Pour the tea into the cup already partially filled with watermelon juice and serve.

FRUIT ICES

Fruit ices are a great way to cool down on a hot day. These versions, like the other Fresh Fruit Quarters, have much less sugar than normal ices so you can spoil yourself and the kids by having more of them! You will be surprised how much flavour these fruit ices give, especially when crunched rather than just sucked.

Oranges and Lemons

5 g lemon verbena
250 ml/8½ oz. freshly squeezed orange juice (ideally without too much pulp)
750 ml/25 oz. water

Makes 4 servings

Place the lemon verbena leaves in a 1 litre/33¾ oz. jug/pitcher or carafe. Briefly blanch the tea with hot water and pour off all the liquid, leaving the leaves in the jug/pitcher.

Add the orange juice, top up with the water and stir the infusion.

Put the jug/pitcher in the refrigerator and allow it to infuse overnight or for about 8 hours

Strain and pour into popsicle moulds and freeze for a few hours or overnight.

Apple Oolong

15 g green oolong
250 ml/8½ oz. freshly pressed sweet apple juice
750 ml/25 oz. water

Makes 4 servings

Put the green oolong tea in a 1 litre/33¾ oz. jug/pitcher or carafe. Briefly brew/wash with hot water for 30 seconds to open the ball-rolled oolong and pour off all the liquid, leaving just the leaves in the jug/pitcher.

Add the sweet apple juice, top up with the water and stir the infusion.

Put the jug/pitcher in the refrigerator and allow it to infuse overnight or for about 8 hours.

Strain and pour into popsicle moulds and freeze for a few hours or overnight.

Watermelon Oolong

15–20 g Oriental Beauty Oolong
250 ml/8½ oz. freshly pressed watermelon juice
750 ml/25 oz. water

Makes 4 servings

Place the Oriental Beauty Oolong in a 1 litre/33¾ oz. jug/pitcher or carafe.

Add the watermelon juice, top up with the water and stir the infusion.

Put the vessel in the refrigerator and allow it to infuse overnight or for about 8 hours.

Strain and pour into popsicle moulds and freeze for a few hours or overnight.

Grapefruit Jasmine

12–15 g jasmine tea
250 ml/8½ oz. freshly pressed
pink grapefruit juice
750 ml/25 oz. water

Makes 4 servings

Put the jasmine tea in a 1 litre/
33¾ oz. jug/pitcher or carafe.
Add the pink grapefruit juice,
top up with the water and stir.

Put the jug/pitcher in the
refrigerator and allow it to infuse
overnight or for about 8 hours.

Strain and pour into popsicle
moulds and freeze for a few
hours or overnight.

5

STONEGROUND TEA
CONTEMPORARY WHISKED TEA

After the Chinese people switched to drinking leaf teas in the Ming dynasty, whisked ground teas slowly disappeared from China but luckily for us this style of tea had already found a home among the tea masters and monks of Japan. Here matcha (which literally means whisked or whipped) tea became central to the Japanese tea ceremony and slowly developed into the vivid green tea we know today. In the 20th century matcha also became a popular culinary ingredient used in numerous drinks and desserts. Recently other kinds of stoneground teas like Hojicha have become more widely available so there has never been a better time to enjoy them instead of using tea syrups and powders that are often stuffed with sugars and other additives.

STONEGROUND MILK TEA

Milk is an interesting medium to bring the joys of stoneground tea to more people as it is the way many prefer to drink their tea, and indeed coffee. Non-dairy milks like soya, almond, rice or coconut milk also work wonderfully with stoneground tea. Iced versions are great, too, when you want something cooling.

Stoneground Milk Tea

8 g stoneground tea
70 ml/2⅓ oz. warm water
570 ml/20 oz. whole milk or 550 ml/19 oz.
dairy-free milk

Makes 4 servings

Whisk the stoneground tea with the warm water in glass jug/pitcher.

Put the mixture into a bottle with a cap and add your choice of milk. Replace the cap and shake briefly.

Warm and whisk as much of the milk tea as you want to drink in a pan to a maximum temperature of 65°C/150°F.

Keep any leftover milk tea refrigerated and use within a day.

Iced Stoneground Milk Tea

8 g stoneground tea
70 ml/2⅓ oz. warm water
570 ml/20 oz. whole milk or 550 ml/19 oz.
dairy-free milk

Makes 4 servings

Whisk the stoneground tea with the warm water in glass jug/pitcher.

Put the mixture into a bottle with a cap and add your choice of milk. Replace the cap and shake briefly.

Refrigerate the mixture and use within a day.

Before serving shake the bottle gently, pour out the tea and serve with ice if required.

MATCHA

Tea has a remarkable ability to transform itself from being an exotic foreign luxury to an intrinsic part of the culture of a country. Nowhere is this more the case than Japan. It is almost impossible to think of Japan and not be reminded of images of a bullet train with Mount Fuji in the background and a green tea field in the foreground or a woman in a kimono whisking a ceremonial bowl of matcha green tea. The tea ceremony, known in Japan as chanoyu, and the arts associated with it are recognized both in Japan and around the world as offering a unique insight into the nation's aesthetic, maybe even its soul. It is indicative of its cultural importance within Japan itself that the government has designated eight tea bowls national treasures and five of them came from China.

In the 13th century whisked tea, which had arrived with Buddhists returning from studying Zen in China, became popular amongst monks who used it as an aid to stay awake and alert during meditation. Soon the warrior class was also enjoying this new style of tea at more luxurious and more raucous tea gatherings. However a new political scene in the 16th century, combined with two remarkable historical figures, crystallized Japanese whisked tea into something more significant.

Matcha is made by stone grinding a shade-grown green tea. Traditionally the grinding was done by hand but today almost all is done by electric stone grinding machines (left).

Sen no Rikyu (1522–1591) was born into a merchant family in the port city of Sakai, near Osaka and not far from the capital Kyoto. After studying tea and Zen from an early age, he became the tea master and confidant of one of Japan's most charismatic leaders, Toyotomi Hideyoshi. Both men were outsiders from humble backgrounds but through their vision and forceful personalities they were able to change the country; Hideyoshi by uniting the nation militarily and Rikyu – with Hideyoshi's patronage – by establishing Wabicha or Rustic Tea as the dominant form of tea and aesthetic. Wabicha's philosophy was expressed through a short meal that preceded the tea, the introduction of more rustic Japanese and Korean tea utensils, small 'mountain hut' like tearooms which were conceived as sanctuaries in the cities, and simple displays of Zen calligraphy and flowers. João Rodrigues, a Jesuit missionary who witnessed tea ceremonies during this time and almost definitely met Sen no Rikyu as he was one of Hideyoshi's interpreters, wrote this description of a 16th century tearoom:

'Emphasis is laid on a frugal and an apparently natural setting; nothing fashionable or elegant is used, but only utensils in keeping with a hermit's retreat. Social distinctions are not observed in this wholesome pastime, and a lower-ranking person may invite a lord or a noble, who on such occasions will behave as an equal. Although usually situated near a mansion or house, the teahouse should be located in a solitary and quiet place'.

Rikyu emphasized this sense of equality by making the entrance to his tearoom tiny so everyone had to crawl to enter, even Hideyoshi who, like other warriors had to leave his sword outside. Sen no Rikyu was fifteen years older than Hideyoshi and when their seemingly strong relationship soured, Rikyu was ordered to commit suicide and his family banished. Hideyoshi came to regret his decision and after several years he restored the family's land. Today, three branches of his family tea schools – Omote Senke, Ura Senke and Mushanokoji Senke – continue to preserve his vision of tea informed by Rikyu's philosophy of harmony (Wa), respect (Kei), purity (Sei) and tranquillity (Jaku).

TRADITIONAL MATCHA

There are two types of matcha – koicha and usucha, or thick and thin tea. Originally there was only koicha but as the tea ceremony evolved usucha was added and usucha is now what most people think of when matcha is mentioned. Usucha is light foamy tea which is usually served with a wagashi, or Japanese sweet. The sugar of the sweet, which is consumed before drinking the tea, balances the flavours and sweet astringency of the tea. The sweet, the shape and design of the tea bowl, any artwork and the flower chosen for the venue's vase usually reflect the season. Selecting and sharing these seasonal things is a big part of tea's enjoyment for many of the people who take part in tea ceremonies.

A chawan by Matsubayashi Hosai, the sixteenth generation of the Asahiyaki kiln in Uji, near Kyoto (right).

To make great matcha you need to find some fresh matcha. As whisked matcha is technically a suspension not an infusion, it contains more caffeine than infused tea. As you ingest the powdered leaves of the plant rather than just infusing them, you may also decide that buying a matcha grown without agrochemicals is important. Whichever matcha you choose, it should have been recently stoneground and be a vibrant green, not a tired beige colour.

There are different ways to make usucha and if you make it as part of tea ceremony you would make it differently from the way I detail overleaf, but several of the steps are the same. The sift and sieving of the matcha really helps reduce the clumping of matcha that can cause harsh bits in the final tea. If you find my recipe does not work for you, you can also make a paste of the matcha with a little bit of the water and the chasen before pouring in the rest and whisking, which is the way you make koicha.

Usucha

2 g/1½ chashaku scoops matcha powder
70 ml/2⅓ oz. hot water at approx. 80°C/175°F

chasen bamboo whisk
tea bowl
cooling jug

Makes 1 serving

Soak the chasen and tea bowl in warm water for 1–2 minutes.

Sieve/strain the matcha powder into the tea bowl.

Pour freshly boiled water into a cooling jug and reduce the temperature to around 80°C/175°F before pouring into the tea bowl.

Whisk the tea briskly with the chasen as if writing the letter 'm'. Continue to whisk until the tea is thoroughly mixed and there is a foam on the surface of the drink.

Gently whisk the letter 'o' in the top of the tea and serve.

Using a chashaku bamboo scoop to take matcha from a lacquer caddy (left).

Matcha shorts

I love matcha. When I lived in Kyoto 25 years ago
I was lucky enough to briefly study how to be a good
tea ceremony guest at one of the Sen family schools.
When I returned to London I also learnt more from
a friend who had studied tea in Japan for many years
but still I never felt 100 per cent comfortable with
whisking up a bowl of matcha. I don't know whether
it was the difficulty of separating a bowl of matcha
from the complex tea ceremony culture or just my
inferior technique, but my efforts always
disappointed me.

After thinking about what I could change to make
matcha more accessible, I decided to use a smaller
vessel as large bowls tend to make the tea lose heat.
I also reduced the quantity of the water used to
around half the size of a bowl of usucha matcha.
This keeps the water warmer and provides me with
a size I feel comfortable with drinking. It also seems
much easier to whisk.

The informality of a smaller vessel held in one
hand, not two, may also make one more relaxed about
not observing the rituals of the tea ceremony and
help one to concentrate on the simple acts of making
and giving or receiving a great cup of whisked tea.

1 g/¾ chashaku scoop matcha powder
35 ml/1¼ oz. hot water at approx.
80°C/175°F

chasen bamboo whisk
small handless tea cup
cooling jug

Makes 1 serving

Soak the chasen and tea bowl in warm
water for 1–2 minutes.

Sieve/strain the matcha powder into
the tea bowl.

Pour freshly boiled water into a cooling
jug and reduce the temperature to around
80°C/175°F before pouring into the tea bowl.

Whisk briskly with the chasen until the all
the tea is mixed in well and there is a foam
on the surface of the drink.

Prufrock

My second tea company East Teas set up a stand at Borough Food Market in 2000 to sell specialist teas from Japan, Korea, Taiwan and China. Among the many people who helped my business partner Alex and I in the early days were the coffee crew of Gwilym, Jorge and Jeremy from Monmouth Coffee Company. It seems remarkable that today I still know and work with them – Gwilym and Jeremy at Prufrock and Jorge with Rick Wells at Fernandez and Wells.

I remember the excitement of the new wave of coffee shops with Antipodean roots that sprung up around London from mid-noughties onwards. Cafes like Flat White, Taylor Street Baristas, The Espresso Room, Kaffeine, Caravan, Lantana, Workshop, Association Coffee, Prufrock and others helped change Londoners' lifestyles and drinking habits

with their new coffees, fabulous breakfasts and friendly service. Many of them also brought the same attention to detail to tea that they applied to their coffees. Provenance was a pillar of the Third Wave coffee so these cafes cared about how their teas were produced and wanted to share that information with their customers. They also wanted to make a good cup of tea so unlike the coffee chains, they ditched the tea bags and started brewing loose leaf.

Prufrock in particular always took the time to make tea beautifully at their brew bar. However, until recently when I visited Prufrock, I would always order a coffee as it would be criminal not to have a coffee at this legendary cafe which attracts coffee pilgrims from around the world including the writer Malcolm Gladwell, who must have been amused to

see the 10,000 hours sign pointing downstairs to the
shop's coffee training centre. Now instead of coffee,
I order a stonerolled tea. I developed these roasted
stoneground teas to directly rival the appeal of milky
coffees but without the support and advice of friends
within the coffee community I do not think they would
have turned out as well as they have. One of these
friends – Andrew Tolley of Taylor Street Baristas –
has called stonerolled tea 'the future of tea in cafes'.
Obviously I hope it is but the future is not decided by
me but other people, so why not visit Prufrock to see
if you agree. There you will find roasted green, roasted
oolong and roasted black versions exquisitely made
and served in 4, 6 and 8 oz. sizes. Thank you Jeremy
and all at Prufrock for their faith, ideas and the
beautiful execution of these new teas.

6
SOMERSAULTS
ICE CREAMS, FRAPPES + SHAKES

These delicious cold drinks and desserts are called somersaults because they are made by tumbling stoneground tea with other ingredients in a blender. The word was also in my mind as I named them after speaking to my mum about what to do when my son was naughty and she had suggested getting him to do twenty somersaults! Hopefully these little tea treats give you the same buzz and smile you get when you do a series of somersaults outside on grass in the summer.

Almost everyone loves ice cream. My family all adore ice cream and eat it even when it's snowing outside. Much as I like ice cream it can be really difficult to find the real thing made without additives, stabilisers and too much sugar, so when my colleague Alex introduced me to banana ice cream made by just blitzing frozen bananas

in a blender I was smitten. I loved its gentle natural sweetness and its ability to work with stoneground teas as well as cacao to make ice creams with a kick.

Somersaults are super simple and if you have the ingredients (basically frozen bananas, some stoneground tea and anything else you want to add) they are much quicker than walking to the shops to get a tub of the mass-produced stuff. As well as ice creams, somersault frappés and thick milkshakes using either dairy or non-dairy milks are easy to make and very easy to drink.

Do develop your own flavour combinations. Stoneground teas flavour somersault drinks and desserts intensely but they do combine well with other ingredients including many soft fruits, herbs and nuts. Also feel free to use less or more stoneground tea to suit your personal palate.

Matcha is Japan's most famous ice cream flavour and is now widely available outside the country. Matcha is really wonderful in all kinds of confectionery and somersaults are no exception. The vibrant green colour and the sweetness of the banana combined with the refreshing grassiness of the tea are addictive. All the matcha somersaults can be topped with a little matcha sprinkled on top if you want an extra zing.

Matcha Somersault Ice Cream

150 g/5½ oz. ripe bananas
3 g matcha

Makes 1–2 servings

Peel and chop the bananas into 2-cm/¾-in. slices. Put the slices into a freezer bag and put in the freezer overnight.

Take the banana slices out of the freezer and allow them to thaw a little before blending in a powerful pulsating blender with the matcha for at least 1 minute. If the banana gets stuck to the sides of the blender use a wooden spatula to remove it and continue to blend. Blend until you have a smooth consistent texture and colour. If this proves difficult, add a little water.

Scoop out the ice cream and serve with a spoon.

Note: If you prefer a stronger or lighter version adjust the amount of matcha you use accordingly.

Matcha Somersault Frappé

150 g/5½ oz. ripe bananas
100 g/4–6 ice cubes (depending on the size of your ice cubes)
55 ml/2 oz. water
4 g matcha

Makes 1–2 servings

Peel and chop the bananas into 2-cm/¾-in. slices. Put the slices into a freezer bag and put in the freezer overnight.

Take the banana slices out of the freezer and allow to thaw a little. Put the banana slices, ice cubes, water, and matcha into a powerful pulsating blender and blend for at least 1 minute.

Pour into a glass with the help of a spoon or spatula and serve with a spoon or straw, or both!

Matcha Somersault Milkshake

150 g/5½ oz. ripe bananas
100 ml/3½ oz. whole milk or soya milk
4 g matcha

Makes 1–2 servings

Peel and chop the bananas into 2-cm/¾-in. slices. Put the slices into a freezer bag and put in the freezer overnight.

Take the banana slices out of the freezer and allow to thaw a little. Put the banana slices, milk and matcha into a powerful pulsating blender and blend for at least 1 minute.

Pour into a glass and serve with a straw or spoon.

Fresh mint works very well with matcha to give these drinks and desserts a lovely cooling kick on a hot day. To mimic my inspiration for this combination you could also add some dark chocolate chips to the somersault ice cream to create a homemade mint chocolate chip ice cream.

Matcha Mint Somersault Ice Cream

150 g/5½ oz. ripe bananas
3 g matcha
10 medium-large fresh mint leaves
some chocolate chips, to serve

Makes 1–2 servings

Peel and chop the bananas into 2-cm/¾-in. slices. Put the slices into a freezer bag and put in the freezer overnight.

Take the banana slices out of the freezer and allow to thaw a little. Put the banana slices, matcha and fresh mint into a powerful pulsating blender and blend for at least 1 minute.

If the banana gets stuck to the sides of the blender use a wooden spatula to remove it and continue to blend. Blend until you have a smooth consistent texture and colour. If this proves difficult, add a little water.

Scoop out the ice cream and serve with a spoon.

If you want to add chocolate, why not cut up some of your favourite chocolate and sprinkle the bits over the ice cream.

Matcha Mint Somersault Frappé

150 g/5½ oz. ripe bananas
100 g/4–6 ice cubes (depending on the size of your ice cubes)
55 ml/2 oz. water
4 g matcha
10 medium-large fresh mint leaves

Makes 1–2 servings

Peel and chop the bananas into 2-cm/¾-in. slices. Put the slices into a freezer bag and put in the freezer overnight.

Take the banana slices out of the freezer and allow to thaw a little. Put the banana slices, ice cubes, water, matcha and mint into a powerful pulsating blender and blend for at least 1 minute.

Pour into a glass with the help of a spoon or a spatula and serve with a spoon or straw, or both!

Matcha Mint Somersault Milkshake

150 g/5½ oz. ripe bananas
100 ml/3½ oz. whole milk or soya milk
4 g matcha
10 medium-large fresh mint leaves

Makes 1–2 servings

Peel and chop the bananas into 2-cm/¾-in. slices.
Put the slices into a freezer bag and put in the
freezer overnight.

Take the banana slices out of the freezer and allow
to thaw a little. Put the banana slices, milk, matcha
and fresh mint leaves into a powerful pulsating
blender and blend for at least 1 minute.

Pour into a glass and serve with a straw or spoon.

Ten years or so ago, in a Japanese department store, I had my first hojicha soft serve ice cream in a cone. I still remember vividly the rich bitter sweet roasted taste of the tea. Ever since, I have scoured ice cream menus and always asked for it whenever it is available. As stoneground hojicha is becoming popular outside Japan, it is a great time to try making it for yourself as your homemade version will be better than anything you can buy.

Hojicha Somersault Ice Cream

150 g/5½ oz. ripe bananas
3 g stoneground hojicha

Makes 1–2 servings

Peel and chop the bananas into 2-cm/¾-in. slices. Put the slices into a freezer bag and put in the freezer overnight.

Take the banana slices out of the freezer and allow to thaw a little. Put the banana slices and stoneground hojicha into a powerful pulsating blender and blend for at least 1 minute.

If the banana gets stuck to the sides of the blender use a wooden spatula to remove it and continue to blend. Blend until you have a smooth consistent texture and colour. If this proves difficult, add a little water.

Scoop out the ice cream and serve with a spoon.

Note: If you prefer a stronger or lighter version adjust the amount of hojicha you use accordingly.

Hojicha Somersault Frappé

150 g/5½ oz. ripe bananas
100 g/4–6 ice cubes (depending on the size of your ice cubes)
55 ml/2 oz. water
4 g stoneground hojicha

Makes 1–2 servings

Peel and chop the bananas into 2-cm/¾-in. slices. Put the slices into a freezer bag and put in the freezer overnight.

Take the banana slices out of the freezer and allow to thaw a little. Put the banana slices, ice cubes, water and stoneground hojicha into a powerful pulsating blender and blend for at least 1 minute.

Pour into a glass with the help of a spoon or a spatula and serve with a spoon or straw, or both!

Hojicha Somersault Milkshake

150 g/5½ oz. ripe bananas
100 ml/3½ oz. whole milk or soya milk
4 g stoneground hojicha

Makes 1–2 servings

Peel and chop the bananas into 2-cm/¾-in. slices. Put the slices into a freezer bag and put in the freezer overnight.

Take the banana slices out of the freezer and allow to thaw a little. Put the banana slices, milk and stoneground hojicha into a powerful pulsating blender and blend for at least 1 minute.

Pour into a glass and serve with a straw or spoon.

If you are after a healthier chocolate ice cream, frappé or milkshake, look no further than these recipes. Hojicoco is so good as a thick milkshake and frappé, that I hope once you have tried them, you will never go back to the sugary versions sold in cafés and restaurants. If you like a strong chocolate flavour, taste the somersault before you empty your blender so you can add a little more cocoa powder if necessary.

Hojicoco Somersault Ice Cream

150 g/5½ oz. ripe bananas
3 g stoneground hojicha
2 g 100% cocoa powder

Makes 1–2 servings

Peel and chop the bananas into 2-cm/¾-in. slices. Put the slices into a freezer bag and put in the freezer overnight.

Take the banana slices out of the freezer and allow to thaw a little. Put the banana slices, stoneground hojicha and cocoa into a powerful pulsating blender and blend for at least 1 minute.

If the banana gets stuck to the sides of the blender use a wooden spatula to remove it and continue to blend. Blend until you have a smooth consistent texture and colour.

Scoop out the ice cream and serve with a spoon.

Hojicoco Somersault Frappé

150 g/5½ oz. ripe bananas
100 g/4–6 ice cubes (depending on the size of your ice cubes)
55 ml/2 oz. water
3 g stoneground hojicha
2 g 100% cocoa powder

Makes 1–2 servings

Peel and chop the bananas into 2-cm/¾-in. slices. Put the slices into a freezer bag and put in the freezer overnight.

Take the banana slices out of the freezer and allow to thaw a little. Put the banana slices, ice cubes, water, stoneground hojicha and cocoa into a powerful pulsating blender and blend for at least 1 minute.

Pour into a glass with the help of spoon or spatula and serve with a spoon or straw, or both!

Hojicoco Somersault Milkshake

150 g/5½ oz. ripe bananas
100 ml/3½ oz. whole milk or soya milk
3 g stoneground hojicha
2 g 100% cocoa powder

Makes 1–2 servings

Peel and chop the bananas into 2-cm/¾-in. slices. Put the slices into a freezer bag and put in the freezer overnight.

Take the banana slices out of the freezer and allow to thaw a little. Put the banana slices, milk, stoneground hojicha and cocoa into a powerful pulsating blender and blend for at least 1 minute.

Pour into a glass and serve with a straw or spoon.

An even darker roast than hojicha, stoneground roasted black tea packs a punch. I developed stoneground roasted black tea to create a tea that would work as well with milky drinks as coffee does. So it is unsurprising that stoneground roasted black tea shares some of coffee's rich flavours.

Stoneground Roasted Black Somersault Ice Cream

150 g/5½ oz. ripe bananas
3 g stoneground roasted black tea

Makes 1–2 servings

Peel and chop the bananas into 2-cm/¾-in. slices. Put the slices into a freezer bag and put in the freezer overnight.

Take the banana slices out of the freezer and allow to thaw a little. Put the banana slices and the stoneground roasted black tea into a powerful pulsating blender and blend for at least 1 minute.

If the banana gets stuck to the sides of the blender use a wooden spatula to remove it and continue to blend. Blend until you have a smooth consistent texture and colour. If this proves difficult, add a little water.

Scoop out the ice cream and serve with a spoon.

Note: If you prefer a stronger or lighter version adjust the amount of stoneground roasted black tea you use accordingly.

Stoneground Roasted Black Somersault Frappé

150 g/5½ oz. ripe bananas
100 g/4–6 ice cubes (depending on the size of your ice cubes)
55 ml/2 oz. water
4 g stoneground roasted black tea

Makes 1–2 servings

Peel and chop the bananas into 2-cm/¾-in. slices. Put the slices into a freezer bag and put in the freezer overnight.

Take the banana slices out of the freezer and allow to thaw a little. Put the banana slices, ice cubes, water and the stoneground roasted black tea into a powerful pulsating blender and blend for at least 1 minute.

Pour into a glass with the help of spoon or spatula and serve with a spoon or straw, or both!

Stoneground Roasted Black Somersault Milkshake

150 g/5½ oz. ripe bananas
100 ml/3½ oz. whole milk or soya milk
4 g stoneground roasted black tea

Makes 1–2 servings

Peel and chop the bananas into 2-cm/¾-in. slices. Put the slices into a freezer bag and put in the freezer overnight.

Take the banana slices out of the freezer and allow to thaw a little. Put the banana slices, milk and the stoneground roasted black tea into a powerful pulsating blender and blend for at least 1 minute.

Pour into a glass and serve with a straw or spoon.

Even before adding the raisins, the stoneground black has a hint of a rum and raisin flavour but adding raisins to the recipe increases the fruity sweetness and also gives a lovely grape flavour. If you want to explore the rum and raisin theme further you can add some rum, whisky or another alcohol you enjoy but be careful as it can take quite a lot of the alcohol for the taste to come through!

Roasted Black Somersault Fruit & Nut Frappé

150 g/5½ oz. ripe bananas
15 g/⅛ cup cashews
100 g/4–6 ice cubes (depending on the size of your ice cubes)
80 ml/3 oz. water
4 g stoneground roasted black tea
10 g raisins

Makes 1–2 servings

Peel and chop the bananas into 2-cm/¾-in. slices. Put the slices into a freezer bag and put in the freezer overnight.

Take a handful of cashew nuts and put them in a dry frying pan/skillet. Toast them on a medium heat until they become golden.

Take the banana slices out of the freezer and allow to thaw a little. Put all the ingredients into a powerful pulsating blender and blend for at least 1 minute.

Pour into a glass with the help of a spoon or spatula and serve with a spoon or straw, or both!

Roasted Black Somersault Fruit & Nut Milkshake

150 g/5½ oz. ripe bananas
15 g/⅛ cup cashews
100 ml/3½ oz. whole milk or soya milk
4 g stoneground roasted black tea
10 g raisins

Makes 1–2 servings

Peel and chop the bananas into 2-cm/¾-in. slices. Put the slices into a freezer bag and put in the freezer overnight.

Take a handful of cashew nuts and put them in a dry frying pan/skillet. Toast them on a medium heat until they become golden.

Take the banana slices out of the freezer and allow to thaw a little. Put all the ingredients into a powerful pulsating blender and blend for at least 1 minute.

Pour into a glass and serve with a straw or spoon.

Roasted Black Somersault Fruit & Nut Ice Cream

150 g/5½ oz. ripe bananas
15 g/⅛ cup cashews
3 g stoneground roasted black tea
10 g raisins

Makes 1–2 servings

Peel and chop the bananas into 2-cm/¾-in. slices. Put the slices into a freezer bag and put in the freezer overnight.

Take a handful of cashew nuts and put them in a dry frying pan/skillet. Toast them on a medium heat until they become golden. Then with a rolling pin gently crush the nuts.

Take the banana slices out of the freezer and allow to thaw a little. Put all the ingredients except the nuts into a powerful pulsating blender and blend for at least 1 minute.

If the banana gets stuck to the sides of the blender use a wooden spatula to remove it and continue to blend. Blend until you have a smooth consistent texture and colour. If this proves difficult, add a little water. Scoop out the ice cream, sprinkle over the nuts and serve with a spoon.

*Tea field, forest, and mountains
on the island of Yakushima, Japan.*

SELECTING LEAF TEA

Japanese Caravan tea. The recipe for this blend is on page 43 (right).

Before you can make delicious tea you need to buy some delicious tea. The easiest way to find good tea is to first find a good tea merchant. Look for companies that do not sell hundreds of types of tea as these merchants often have a problem with freshness due to the size of their range. Also, unless you are looking for a flavoured tea, avoid tea stores that have a huge selection of flavoured teas because these highly scented teas often taint their non-flavoured teas.

Seek out specialist tea companies that sometimes focus on just one country or region as their passion for good provenance usually shows a passion for good tea. These kinds of companies will have knowledgeable staff who can help you find what you want and recommend the teas they themselves have enjoyed. Although it can be interesting to see and smell the tea leaves, be wary of tea merchants that let you smell their tea from the same large container they sell from as they are exposing their teas constantly to air, light and moisture. On this point make sure that if the tea is pre-packed and sold in a canister or packaging that it is at least airtight and properly sealed.

Make the most of merchants that allow you to taste their teas in store or who will send or sell you small samples. There is nothing more annoying than spending a lot of money on a mediocre tea that you were unable to try, particularly if it is from a famous tea brand where one wonders if you are paying more for the name and the packaging than the tea. For a similar reason, until you know a tea merchant and a particular tea well, try to buy the smallest quantity you can – that way even if you don't love the tea, you can soon finish it.

If you are buying without tasting the tea, the tea label can also be a source of some useful information like the producer's name and the place of origin. Sometimes if the tea is an Indian or Sri Lankan tea, the leaf grade will be on the pack. Leaf grades like Super Fine Tippy Golden Flowery Orange Pekoe (SFTGFOP) – a top leaf grade you often see for Darjeelings – always put me in mind of the Mary Poppin's song *Supercalifragilisticexpialidocious*. Like the song, the leaf grade is a little meaningless because although it may indicate the quality of the leaf it does not guarantee the quality of the taste of the tea – there are many mediocre teas with fancy leaf grades. A label may also tell you which year and season it was produced or when it was blended which gives a good guide to the freshness of the tea.

Organic tea or other kinds of tea produced without agrochemicals may also be indicated by the label. Pesticides and herbicides can be harmful not only to you but also to the people and places that produce tea as they are often applied without proper protection and the chemicals run off into the local water supply. There are other marks and certification schemes which aim to help worker conditions, often on large estates and plantations, but bear in mind that these marks usually do not improve the wages of workers. Buying teas from companies that purchase directly from small family producers who make their tea without hired help may mean more of your money goes back to the producer. If these issues are important to you, don't be afraid to ask a merchant for more details about a tea's provenance and if they cannot or will not tell you more, maybe you would be better off buying your tea elsewhere.

LEAF TEA SELLERS

UK
Canton Tea www.cantonteaco.com

Comins Tea www.cominstea.com

Fortnum & Mason www.fortnumandmason.com

Good and Proper Tea www.goodandpropertea.com

Imperial Teas www.imperialteas.co.uk

Jing Tea www.jingtea.com

Lalani & Co www.lalaniandco.com

My Cup of Tea www.mycupoftea.co.uk

Pekoe Tea www.pekoetea.co.uk

Postcard Teas www.postcardteas.com

Rare Tea Company www.rareteacompany.com

Robert Wilson Ceylon Tea www.wilstea.com

Tiosk www.tiosk.co.uk

Waterloo Tea www.waterlootea.com

What-Cha www.what-cha.com

USA/Canada
Adagio Teas www.adagio.com

Camellia Sinensis www.camellia-sinensis.com

Elmwood Inn store.elmwoodinn.com

Floating Leaves www.floatingleavestea.com

Harney & Sons www.harney.com

In Pursuit of Tea www.inpursuitoftea.com

O5 Tea www.o5tea.com

Red Blossom Tea Company www.redblossomtea.com

Rishi www.rishi-tea.com

Song Tea Ceramics www.songtea.com

T Shop www.tshopny.com

Té Company www.te-nyc.com

Tea Drunk www.tea-drunk.com

Tea Habitat www.teahabitat.com

Teance www.teance.com

Tea Urchin www.teaurchin.com

Upton Tea Imports www.uptontea.com

Asia
Eco Cha www.eco-cha.com

The Essence of Tea www.essenceoftea.com

Floating Leaves www.floatingleavestea.com

Hibiki-An www.hibiki-an.com

Hojo www.hojotea.com

Horaido www.kyoto-teramachi.or.jp/horaido

Ippodo www.ippodo-tea.co.jp

Koyamaen www.marukyu-koyamaen.co.jp

Obubu Tea Farms www.obubutea.com

Rishouen www.rishouentea.com

Sun Sing www.sunsingtea.com

Taiwan Sourcing www.taiwanoolongs.com

Taiwan Tea Crafts www.taiwanteacrafts.com

Tea Masters www.tea-masters.com

The Jade Leaf www.thejadeleaf.com

Thés du Japon www.thes-du-japon.com

Wan Ling Tea House www.wanlingteahouse.com

Yunnan Sourcing www.yunnansourcing.com

Yunomi Tea www.yunomi.life

Yuuki-Cha www.yuuki-cha.com

Europe

Klasek Tea www.darjeeling.cz

Les Jardins de Gaia www.jardinsdegaia.com

Mariage Frères www.mariagefreres.com

Palais des Thés www.palaisdesthes.com

Paper and Tea www.paperandtea.com

Tee Gschwendner www.teegschwendner.de

Teekampagne www.teekampagne.de

Terre de Chine www.terredechine.com

Clockwise from right to left: Tea pickers returning home in Assam, withering trays filled with tea leaves, and tea pickers' baskets hanging in tea trees on Wu Dong mountain in China.

Postcard Teas

When Postcard Teas opened in 2005, it was probably the only specialist tea store in London that did not sell any tea bags. It would have made financial sense to sell some tea bags in a city where almost everyone uses tea bags but we would have had to ditch one of our core beliefs is that leaf tea is better. Over the last 12 years we have not changed the UK's tea-drinking habits but together with other leaf tea companies we have been part of a growing appreciation of leaf tea.

We also hoped to connect our customers to the people and places that make the tea we sell. I have been travelling to tea-growing areas since 1993 but working with Asako and Lu it was possible to develop even stronger relationships with small-scale tea farms of only a few acres in Japan and China. We had a plan to become the first tea company working across Asia to put proper provenance on all of our teas, which we were able to do on our 60 or so teas in 2008. All of us believed this kind of traceability was needed not only for peace of mind but also for connoisseurship. 'Every cup tells a story' is another tea brand's slogan but you can only tell a story or learn something if you know at least the producer's name, the place and the season the tea was made, and ideally much more.

The store is on the ground floor of a three-hundred-year-old building which has previously been a grocery store, a tearoom and an art gallery and in a strange way we combine those strands in what we do. From the beginning we commissioned craftsmen to produce handmade tea ware and utensils and invite them to have exhibitions and do workshops in the space. Takahiro Yagi – the sixth generation craftsman of Kaikado, a company that makes caddies by hand in Kyoto – kindly comes over every year. His

visits are always one of the highlights of our year and our customers love it when he engraves their name in Japanese on his special scoops. The original team has been joined by Jonathan, Alex and Marie who also go to see new tea farms, and tea makers also come to the store to share their knowledge. These forms of communication and interaction are what we aim for so it is unsurprising that our company name is Postcard Teas, representing both our travels and our aim to share our love of leaf tea with more people. Indeed one of the most popular formats of our tea is a box which can be written on and sent like a postcard. Slowly spreading the word and leaf tea!

This page, clockwise from top: a vintage Kaikado tin caddy, a new Kaikado tin caddy made for Postcard Teas, shelves of tea ware, a couple writing tea postcards to friends. Opposite page: Postcard Teas' dark green façade is one of the few surviving original storefronts in the Bond Street area of Mayfair.

INDEX

ACKNOWLEDGMENTS

I would like to thank Asako and my family in the UK and
Japan for all their love and support. Also my Postcard Teas'
colleagues, especially Lu, Jonathan, Alex and Marie for
their ideas and contributions. And the creative team of
Jan, Lesley and Peter have been a pleasure to work with
and I am extremely grateful for their brilliance and diligence.
Many thanks are due to Suresh for being a great agent and
introducing me to the lovely crew at RPS. Thank you Cindy,
Leslie, Julia, Megan and Miriam. Finally thanks to Jeremy
Lee, Jeremy Challender and Raphaël Rodriguez for their
warm hospitality. Further thanks to Vaughn who helped
define ambient tea.

Senior designer Megan Smith
Editor Miriam Catley
Production Mai-Ling Collyer
Art director Leslie Harrington
Editorial director Julia Charles
Publisher Cindy Richards
Photography art director and
  prop stylist Lesley Dilcock
Indexer Vanessa Bird

First published in 2017 by
Ryland Peters & Small
20–21 Jockey's Fields,
London WC1R 4BW
and
341 E 116th St, New York NY 10029
www.rylandpeters.com

10 9 8 7 6 5 4 3 2 1

Text copyright © Timothy d'Offay 2017

Design and photographs copyright ©
Ryland Peters & Small 2017
Photography on pages 23, 24, 25, 58,
134–5, 139 © Timothy d'Offay 2017

ISBN: 978-1-84975-824-6

Printed in China

Note
British (Metric) and American
(Imperial ounce and fluid ounce)
measurements are included for your
convenience, however it is important
to work with one set of measurements
and not alternate between the two
within a recipe. Where very small
measurements occur, they have
been provided in grams where there
is no suitable Imperial conversion.

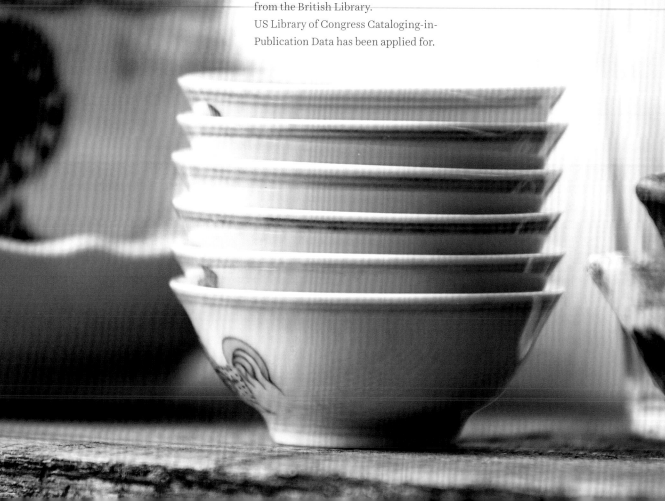